Catholic Theological Formation Series

General Editor: Kevin Zilverberg

The Catholic Theological Formation Series is sponsored by The Saint Paul Seminary School of Divinity, the graduate school of theological formation for Roman Catholic seminarians and laity enrolled at the University of Saint Thomas in Saint Paul, Minnesota. As a premier institution of theological formation for the region and beyond, The Saint Paul Seminary School of Divinity seeks to form men and women for the task of fulfilling the specific call God has for them, a call grounded in their common baptismal vocation to serve one another in Christ.

As an institution of the Archdiocese of Saint Paul and Minneapolis, the school is intentional in its commitment to priestly formation for the archdiocese and the broader region. As an institution of graduate theological education, the school prepares the laity for the equally compelling task of making Christ known and loved in the world. Though distinct in their various ministries, the common goal of intense theological formation is shared across the curriculum.

It is this challenge of theological formation—the challenge to faithfully inform one's understanding—that serves as the focus of this series, with special attention given to the task of preparing priests, teachers, and leaders within the Roman Catholic tradition. Although the series is academic in tenor, it aims beyond mere academics in its intellectual approach. We seek to promote a form of discourse that is professional in its conduct and spiritual in its outcomes, for theological formation is more than an exercise in academic technique. It is rather about the perfecting of a spiritual capacity: the capacity on the part of the human person to discern what is true and good.

This series, then, aims to develop the habits of mind required of a sound intellect—a spiritual aptitude for the truth of God's living Word and his Church. Most often, it will draw from the more traditional specializations of historical, systematic, moral, and biblical scholarship. Homiletics and pastoral ministry are anticipated venues as well. There will be occasions, however, when a theme is examined across disciplines and periods, for the purposes of bringing to our common consideration a thesis yet undeveloped.

Despite the variety of methodologies and topics explored, the series' aim remains constant: to provide a sustained reflection upon the mission and ministry of Catholic theological formation of both priests and laity alike.

The general editor of the Catholic Theological Formation Series, Fr. Kevin Zilverberg, serves as assistant professor of sacred Scripture and the founding director of Saint Paul Seminary Press at The Saint Paul Seminary School of Divinity.

Piercing the Clouds

Lectio Divina *and Preparation for Ministry*

Edited by

Kevin Zilverberg and Scott Carl

SAINT PAUL
SEMINARY PRESS

SAINT PAUL, MINNESOTA • 2021

Cover image from Wikimedia Commons: An Angel with the Eternal Gospel (Rev 14:6ff);
Ms. Ludwig III 1 (83.MC.72), fol. 27; The J. Paul Getty Museum
Cover design by Willem Mineur

Published 2021 by
Saint Paul Seminary Press
2260 Summit Ave., Saint Paul, Minnesota 55105

Library of Congress Control Number: 2021933314
LC record available at https://lccn.loc.gov/2021933314

Catholic Theological Formation Series

ISSN 2765-9283
ISBN 978-1-953936-04-2 (paperback)
ISBN 978-1-953936-54-7 (ebook)

www.spspress.com

Contents

Abbreviations

ACW	Ancient Christian Writers
AncB	Anchor Bible
BECNT	Baker Exegetical Commentary on the New Testament
BNTC	Black's New Testament Commentary
CCSSc	Catholic Commentary on Sacred Scripture
CSEL	Corpus Scriptorum Ecclesiasticorum Latinorum
CTFS	Catholic Theological Formation Series
CWS	Classics of Western Spirituality
DSBP	Dizionario di Spiritualità Biblico-Patristica
EnchBib	Enchiridion Biblicum
ESEC	Emory Studies in Early Christianity
GBSNT	Guides to Biblical Scholarship, New Testament Series
ICC	International Critical Commentary
Int.	Interpretation
JSNTS	*Journal for the Study of the New Testament*, Supplement Series
LThPM	Louvain Theological and Pastoral Monographs
NABRE	New American Bible, revised edition
NAC	New American Commentary
NICNT	New International Commentary on the New Testament
NJB	New Jerusalem Bible
NPNF	Nicene and Post-Nicene Fathers
PG	Patrologia Graeca
PL	Patrologia Latina
RGPs	Revised Grail Psalms
RSV	Revised Standard Version
SaPaSe	Sacra Pagina Series
SC	Sources Chrétiennes
SFSHJ	South Florida Studies in the History of Judaism
SJ(L)	Studies in Judaism (Lanham)
SubBi	Subsidia Biblica
TB	Theologische Bücherei
WBC	Word Biblical Commentary
WUNT	Wissenschaftliche Untersuchungen zum Neuen Testament

Introduction

Our earliest description of a four-step *lectio divina* (spiritual or "divine" reading) conceives of the steps as so many rungs of a ladder reaching up into the heavens. Carthusian Prior Guigo II wrote this description, in which he develops his metaphor of the ladder: "It has few rungs, yet its length is immense and wonderful, for its lower end rests upon the earth, but its top pierces the clouds and touches heavenly secrets."[1] Nearly everyone who has heard of *lectio divina* has learned Guigo's four steps for the prayerful reading of sacred Scripture: *lectio, meditatio, oratio,* and *contemplatio* (reading, meditation, prayer, and contemplation). Even so, Guigo does not insist upon the ladder but hastens to add another metaphor, that of taste.[2] Upon reaching the ladder's *contemplatio* rung, the mind has ascended so high that "it tastes the joys of everlasting sweetness."[3]

To use Guigo's language, this book's six essays pertain to the "piercing of the clouds," which characterizes *lectio divina* practiced well. Furthermore, the essays give special attention to the practice of *lectio divina* during preparation for ministry, especially the ministry of Catholic priests. That being said, any current or prospective Bible-reader can profit from this book; most of its content applies not only to Catholic seminarians, but to literate Christians in general.

1. Guigo II, *Ladder of Monks* 2, trans. Edmund Colledge and James Walsh, in *The Ladder of Monks and Twelve Meditations* (Kalamazoo, MI: Cistercian Publications, 1981), p. 68.

2. Daniel Keating, "*Oratio* and *Contemplatio* (and *Actio*) of *Lectio Divina*," 98–110, at 100 of the present volume.

3. Guigo II, *Ladder of Monks* 2, p. 68.

Each of the six authors presented a preliminary version of his essay during the conference "Exegesis, *Lectio Divina*, and the Ministry of the Word," held June 7–9, 2017 at The Saint Paul Seminary (University of St. Thomas in St. Paul, Minnesota). My colleague and coeditor, Scott Carl, organized and hosted this conference, which was sponsored by the Msgr. Jerome D. Quinn Institute for Biblical Studies. At that time, Carl was director of the institute, and I assisted him in his duties as host. He took responsibility for selecting the speakers (and other participants), who came by invitation only. Carl then began the editorial process as the sole editor, selecting certain conference essays for publication and sending each of them to a single reviewer for double-blind peer review. Carl's increased administrative responsibilities at the seminary, however, prevented him from advancing the project. Therefore, I took over editorial responsibility at the same time that I assumed Carl's former position as director of the Quinn Institute in the summer of 2019. Since then, the institute has been renamed as an endowment, one of several that fund the Institute for Catholic Theological Formation at our seminary. Since I am the director of this new institute, I continue to oversee the Quinn Endowment, which has sponsored this book's publication.[4]

When I acquired the essays from Carl, he had already received the blind reviewers' approvals for each one. I read the essays critically and requested further editing by each author, though I judged some chapters to need only the smallest of adjustments. I commend all the authors for their willingness to revise their essays long after composing them, and for their humility in accepting corrections (more often, suggestions) from the reviewers and me. Their commitment to scholarship, which in the summer of 2017 enriched a score of biblical professors teaching in Catholic seminaries, now stands to benefit a larger audience and to make a lasting impact on the Church. It is my honor, now, to summarize each of their essays.

Laurence Kriegshauser, OSB, has contributed the first chapter, titled "Western Monastic Tradition of *Lectio Divina* and Seminary Formation." He devotes the longest section of his three-part essay to the history of *lectio divina*, beginning with the reception of sacred Scripture in the early Christian liturgical assembly. Kriegshauser proceeds to highlight third-century Fathers who encouraged extra-liturgical Scripture reading and reflection, a practice that continued to develop as the eremitical life and monasticism flourished as paths

4. I would like to take this opportunity to thank my editing and production team for their work on this volume: Erika Zabinski, copyeditor and indexer; Maggee Becker, proofreader; and Judy Gilats, typesetter. Your skills and diligence are appreciated.

to Christian perfection. Eventually, Benedict of Nursia and others established monastic rules that inculcated the prayerful reading of Scripture, especially the Psalms. *Lectio divina* finally gained its classical formulation, which can be traced as far back as the Carthusian Prior Guigo II in the late twelfth century: *lectio, meditatio, oratio, contemplatio* (reading, meditation, prayer, contemplation). Kriegshauser completes the historical arc of *lectio divina* by pointing out salient developments in the late Middle Ages, through the modern period, and up until the present day. In the second part of his essay he describes the characteristics of *lectio divina*. A survey of diverse but complementary definitions by Louis Bouyer, Charles Dumont, Blessed Columba Marmion, Mariano Magrassi, and C. Jean-Nesmy suggest that this practice, which aims at personal union with God, cannot be definitively captured in any one description. Nevertheless, Kriegshauser helpfully distills four dimensions of *lectio divina*: it is 1) affective, engaging "the whole person, mind and heart, soul and body";[5] 2) relational, between the reader and the Lord; 3) transformative for the reader; and 4) ecclesial, building on the foundation of sacred history. In the third and final part of this chapter, Kriegshauser addresses the use of *lectio divina* in seminary formation, especially the experience at Kenrick-Glennon Seminary in St. Louis, Missouri. His description and honest assessment of practices will help other teachers and students to think about *lectio divina* in their own communities. As with *lectio divina* itself, which Kriegshauser humbly refrains from simplifying into a spiritual algorithm, so too he refrains from proposing a single formula for every seminary to implement.

Michael Magee surveys the treatment of John 6 in commentaries by Rudolf Bultmann (first edition by Bultmann in 1941), Rudolf Schnackenburg (first edition for John 5–12 in 1971), and coauthors Francis Martin and William F. Wright IV (2015), in his chapter "The Implications of Exegetical Method for *Lectio Divina*: John 6 as Treated in Three Commentaries." Magee recognizes the need for a commentary to treat not only the historical critical dimension of the biblical text, but also the "second methodological level,"[6] which takes into account the unity of all of sacred Scripture and the Church's living tradition. Although Bultmann does recognize the biblical text (in this case, John 6) as presenting a spiritual challenge to the reader, Magee ultimately concludes that this commentary is ill-suited for *lectio divina*. Bultmann's reordering of the text, and his conclusion that it contains passages which significantly distort Jesus' message, suggest that it would be inappropriate for the practitioner

5. P. 22.
6. Pp. 31–32.

of *lectio divina* to read and reflect on John 6 in its canonical form in order to assimilate Jesus' message. Magee finds Schnackenburg's commentary less extreme in its reordering of John 6 and welcomes the attempt to integrate results of critical biblical studies into his confessional, Catholic interpretative framework. These characteristics suggest that this commentary provides a better preparation for *lectio divina* than does Bultmann's, but one may be disappointed in Schnackenburg's failure, in his treatment of John 6, to spiritually challenge the reader. The commentary by Martin and Wright devotes less attention to redaction criticism, but it does not reject historical critical analysis of the text. This commentary's orientation toward a less specialized audience, its willingness to treat the text in its canonical form, its acknowledgment of a single divine author of all Scripture, and its greater emphasis on situating John 6 within the broader Catholic tradition all recommend it for use in *lectio divina*.

Konrad Schaefer, OSB, contributed the chapter "*Lectio Divina* Fosters Growth and Formation."[7] In the first half of this two-part essay, Schaefer provides the theological underpinnings for the practice of *lectio divina*. This prayerful approach to Scripture corresponds to its divine authorship; it would be inappropriate to focus exclusively on the human aspect of biblical literature without ever praying over it. A prayerful approach, however, does not exclude but rather complements biblical interpretation according to the historical critical method. Schaefer demands more of the reader than blind faith or cold textual analysis: he calls for "historical criticism complemented by friendship with God."[8] In the second half of Schaefer's essay, he turns to more practical considerations for fostering *lectio divina* among students, especially candidates for the Catholic priesthood. For example, appreciation of reading in general disposes the student to appreciate the Bible. Moreover, we possess within our Judeo-Christian tradition models for fruitful Bible reading, such as midrashic re-reading of a biblical text, which discovers in the text new meaning and relevance within the reader's circumstances and cultural milieu. What does Nehemiah 8 narrate but the "exuberant collegial *lectio divina* on the day of the consecration of the new temple"? Since re-readings occur already within the Bible,

7. The chapter in this volume has some content that also appears in "*Divina lectio* y formación humana," by the same author, which appeared in *Efemérides Mexicana* 36, no. 106 (2018): 68–113. Nevertheless, the essay in the present volume differs from the Spanish one in much more than just its language of composition. Some of the topics treated are simply different. Furthermore, Schaefer revised the English essay according to my recommendations, after the Spanish one had already been published.

8. Pp. 60–64.

the contemporary interpreter can take a cue from the biblical text itself and make his or her own re-readings. Finally, the second half of the essay culminates in Schaefer's proposal for a "*lectio* seminar," which consists of prayerful group reading of the Sunday lectionary.

Marcin Kowalski uses the test case of Romans 7:7–25 to illustrate the importance of an objectively grounded reading of sacred Scripture for the meditation stage of *lectio divina,* in his chapter "*Meditatio* of *Lectio Divina* Following upon Exegesis-Informed *Lectio*: The Test Case of Romans 7:7–25." This passage, within a larger section on the fruits of justification (Romans 5–8), strikes a tone of desperation, in which Paul writes, "Wretched man that I am! Who will deliver me from this body of death?" (7:24 RSV). Kowalski summarizes the many scholarly attempts to identify the *ego* of this apparently interruptive passage: Is it Paul? Israel? the Adamic *ego*? the Christian *ego*? Readers of Romans 7:7–25 tend to associate themselves personally with the sinful paralysis of the one who does not the good that one wants to do, but the evil that one detests (7:19); they implicitly identify the *ego* here as the Christian *ego.* Such an exegetically uninformed *lectio,* however, distorts one's *meditatio.* Kowalski avails himself of rhetorical criticism to explain why Romans 7:7–25 should instead be considered one of three proofs for establishing the contrast between sinful man and free humanity. By ruling out the common interpretation that this passage describes the Christian *ego* paralyzed by sin, Kowalski shows how these verses lead not so much to lamentation as to thanksgiving. A *lectio* of Romans 7:7–25 informed in this way leads the prayerful reader "to praise God for the undeserved and super-generous gift of new life in Christ which liberates us from the tyranny of Law and sin."[9]

Daniel Keating addresses the final stages of *lectio divina* in his chapter "*Oratio* and *Contemplatio* (and *Actio*) of *Lectio Divina.*" He takes as his starting point Pope Benedict XVI's teaching on *lectio divina* as presented in the post-synodal apostolic exhortation on the word of God in the life and mission of the Church, *Verbum Domini.*[10] Keating describes the earliest known presentation of the classical four stages of *lectio divina,* by Guigo II. Guigo's focus on the affective response to Bible reading put monks on guard against a merely rational reading of Scripture, an arid exercise. This would make his work popular in the Devotio Moderna of later centuries and, in fact, finds an echo in Benedict's own concerns. Both these men agree on the transformative nature

9. P. 97.

10. Pope Benedict XVI, *Verbum Domini* (September 30, 2010) (Boston: Pauline Books and Media, 2010), §82 and §86–87.

of *oratio*, but Benedict's description takes greater account of the variety of prayer beyond one's affective response. Furthermore, the pope's description of *contemplatio* contrasts with that of the monk. Benedict's terms of "vision" and "seeing" suggest the lively engagement of the intellect, whereas Guigo put the emphasis on the affective metaphor of "taste." Keating concludes by treating *actio* (action), a final step of *lectio divina* in addition to the classical fourfold description. Although Benedict adds *actio* without much description, Keating builds upon the thoughts of Augustine, Gregory the Great, and Thomas Aquinas to elaborate its place in *lectio divina.* A healthy tension between dedicating one's time to quiet contemplation and to activity in the service of one's neighbor ultimately reveals that *lectio divina* culminates in *actio*, and *actio* leaves the Christian needing to return to scriptural prayer for refreshment and renewed strength.

Anthony Giambrone, OP, transcends the boundaries of *lectio*, *meditatio*, *oratio*, and *contemplatio* in his contribution, "*Exquisitio, Supplicatio, Praedicatio*: Searching the Scriptures and the Mystery of Preaching." He advocates for saturation in sacred Scripture within Catholic seminaries, taking the post-Tridentine English College at Douay as a model. Giambrone recognizes, nevertheless, the greatly changed circumstances since then, in biblical studies and in the world. Critical commentaries do indeed enrich our *lectio* nowadays, but Giambrone warns against reliance on commentaries that engage the biblical text scientifically without ever arriving at the divinely revealed truths contained therein. Fruitful *lectio* requires prayer and meditation on the mysteries of sacred theology in addition to diligent study; this very sort of integration of the sacred page into the whole of the priestly formation program at Douay challenges our present-day paradigms. There, scriptural debate in the classroom fits into a larger theological and evangelical enterprise sustained by the reading of Scripture in one's own quarters, in the refectory, and in the chapel. Giambrone proceeds to discuss the transition from *lectio* to *oratio*: for him, the more robust alternatives to these two terms are *exquisitio* (the "searching" of the sacred text) and *supplicatio* (the "supplication" or prayer life of the reader). The early Church fathers and later Christian writers will inform these activities and allow the reader to assimilate time-tested spiritual readings. Finally, the priest culminates his *exquisitio* and *supplicatio* in *praedicatio* (preaching), which provides a practical focus and an eschatological terminus for *lectio divina.*

Guigo II provided a starting point for the description of *lectio divina* and the piercing of the clouds. The preceding summaries show how this book, in some ways, consolidates that tradition. Even more so, however, these essays develop the Catholic tradition of prayerful Bible reading; they point the way to new, creative readings within the framework of a time-honored approach. Let this book serve as a stimulus to maintain and develop the practice of *lectio divina* in seminaries and in the whole Church. This can only redound to the praise of Jesus' name by Bible-immersed ministers of the Church and the lay faithful who follow their lead.

Fr. Kevin Zilverberg
November 21, 2020

Western Monastic Tradition of *Lectio Divina* and Seminary Formation

Laurence Kriegshauser, OSB

History

Lectio divina is an encounter with the person of the risen Lord Jesus who speaks to us in the sacred word. The Bible is the record of God's dealings with men, culminating in the mystery of the death and resurrection of his divine Son made flesh. The two parts of the Christian Bible recount the long preparation of the people of God for a Messiah and the appearance of that Messiah in Jesus of Nazareth. The Old Testament reveals the Creator's intention of drawing and uniting mankind to himself. The New Testament, composed in a much shorter time span, records the life of Christ and his significance for the first Christian communities. Inspired by the Spirit of God, these writings constitute a definitive presentation of that which God wished to be known by his people for their salvation. Since the essence of that message is not merely an idea or a truth or a history, but a living person, the Son of God made man, living forever as God and man at the right hand of the Father, the reading of the texts that enclose this message actually makes him present. The reading of the inspired word is a meeting between the Christian believer and the Lord in whom he believes.

The place of the Scriptures is in the Church, the assembly gathered for worship. It is in the Church that the word of God is proclaimed and received by the community. The word can be said to make the community, since it is by faith in the Lord preached by the first witnesses and recorded in the Scriptures that the assembly is constituted.[1] The word proclaimed in the community flows

1. Pope Benedict XVI, *Verbum Domini* (September 30, 2010) (Washington, DC: United States Conference of Catholic Bishops, 2010), §50–51.

immediately into the communal act of worship which is the offering of the sacrifice of Jesus to the Father and the sacramental communion of the faithful in the Body and Blood of the Lord. The proclamation of the word can be seen as an integral part, an initial stage, of the Eucharistic sacrifice which makes the assembly into the Body of Christ.[2] The essential purpose of the sacred Scriptures is to fill the believing community with the saving knowledge of the risen Lord. Word and Eucharist together build the Church.

Historically, part of the Church's liturgical worship was the commenting on the sacred readings by the presider of the ceremony. Such commentary showed how the texts that had been read contribute to the understanding of the Christ mystery, the focal point of all the Scriptures. Such elucidation of the divine word would kindle the hearts of the assembly and provoke them to offer themselves to the Father along with the memorial offering of the sacrifice of Christ. In the early centuries after Christ, homilies on the scriptural readings began to be recorded. As teachers and catechists meditated on the mysteries hidden in the biblical books, they helped their congregations probe more deeply into the mystery of Christ, his wondrous saving acts, his teaching, and his present activity in the Church through the action of the Holy Spirit. It became clear that the principal means for deepening one's knowledge of and intimacy with Christ was to read and reflect on the Scriptures. Saint Jerome, the Doctor of the Scriptures, would say famously, "Ignorance of the Scriptures is ignorance of Christ."[3]

In the third century CE, Christian writers began to exhort the faithful to undertake reading the sacred writings outside the liturgy. Very early this process of personal reading of the Scriptures was termed *lectio divina*, divine reading, a term referring both to the text itself—divine because inspired by the Holy Spirit and revealing the divine plan—and to the process of reading this sacred text.[4] Manuscripts of these readings, of the Old and New Testaments or parts

2. According to Karl Rahner, "Grace is always in the form of the word: grace is present always and everywhere from beginning to end, from the first word of preaching to the sacrament inclusively, in the form of the word." "The Word and the Eucharist," 253–286 in *Theological Investigations*, vol. 4 (Baltimore: Helicon Press, 1966), 286, cited in Daniel Shin, "Some Light from Origen: Scripture as Sacrament," *Worship* 73, no. 5 (September 1999): 399–425, at 415–416.

3. Jerome, *In Isaiam*, Prologue (PL 24, 17). All nonbiblical translations are my own unless otherwise noted.

4. The Greek term equivalent to *lectio divina*, θεία ἀνάγνωσις, is found already in Origen, e.g., *Letter to Gregory Thaumaturgus* 4 (PG 11, 92).

of these, would not have been easily available.[5] Those with access to scrolls or codices would undertake to memorize important passages or whole books of the Bible.[6] Their prayer would be centered on the divine word and the encounter with the person contained in the word. Origen (d. 254) earnestly promoted the personal study of the Scriptures by the Christian faithful, urging them to return each day to the wells of sacred Scripture like Rebecca.[7] Daily reading of Scripture was a prolongation of the hearing of the word in the liturgy.

The practice of personal meditation on the sacred writings had its counterpart and root in Judaism. According to Psalm 1, the just man is one who "murmurs his Law day and night" (Ps 1:2 NJB), that is, recites to himself continually the divine word, particularly the psalms. The passion for the divine word and for constant intercourse with it animates Psalm 119: "With my lips have I recounted the decrees of your mouth" (Ps 119:13 RGPs); "In your commands I have found my delight; these I have loved" (119:47); "How sweet is your promise to my tongue, more than honey in the mouth" (119:103). Christian writers were soon applying such verses to the Christian's loving interaction with the word of God in both Testaments. Saint Ambrose wrote a masterful treatise on Psalm 119, showing how each of its 176 verses could be prayed by the Christian.[8] In his

5. However, the Scillitan martyrs (180 CE) had in their possession copies of the Gospels and the Letters of Paul. André Boland, "*Lectio divina* et lecture spirituelle," 470–510 in *Dictionnaire de spiritualité: Ascétique et mystique, doctrine et histoire*, vol. 9, ed. Marcel Viller, Ferdinand Cavallera, and Joseph de Guilbert (Paris: Beauchesne, 2018), 473.

6. It would be said of Anthony of Egypt that "he was so attentive at the reading of the Scripture lessons that nothing escaped him: he retained everything and so his memory served him in place of books." Athanasius, *Life of Anthony*, trans. Robert T. Meyer (Westminster, MD: The Newman Press, 1950), section 3, p. 21.

7. Origen, *Homilies on Genesis*, trans. Ronald E. Heine, *Homilies on Genesis and Exodus* (Washington, DC: Catholic University of America Press, 1982), homily 10 (on Gen 24:15–16), section 2, p. 160.

8. For example, Ambrose interprets Psalm 119:92, "If your law had not been my meditation, then I might have perished in my affliction," in the light of Paul's teaching on spiritual warfare: "Therefore in time of affliction when we are crushed with adversity, our meditation should be on the law, lest the whirlwind of temptation overcome us in its attack. An athlete will not enter into competition unless he has first practiced in the gymnasium. Let us therefore anoint the limbs of our minds with the oil of reading. Let us exercise ourselves day and night in the gymnasium of the divine Scriptures; may the healthy food of spiritual refreshment strengthen our spiritual limbs, so that when the devil begins his attack, throwing the dust of temptation into our face, we may stand unafraid, striving without wavering and not beating the air. . . . Let us therefore exercise ourselves by continual meditation; let us exercise ourselves before battle so that we are always prepared for battle." *Expositio in Psalmum CXVIII*, book 12, section 28 (PL 15, 1442).

commentary on Psalm 1 he explicitly identifies the Law on which the psalmist meditates as Christ:

> Drink therefore from each cup, the Old and New Testament; because in each you drink Christ. Drink Christ because he is the vine; drink Christ because he is the rock which gave forth water; drink Christ because he is the fount of life; drink Christ because he is the river whose waters give joy to God's city; drink Christ because he is peace; drink Christ because rivers of living water flow from his side; drink Christ that you may drink the blood by which you are redeemed; drink Christ so that you may drink his words; his word is the Old Testament, his word is the New Testament. Divine Scripture is drunk and divine Scripture is eaten when into the veins of the mind and the powers of the soul the juice [*succus*] of the eternal word descends. Finally, not on bread alone does man live but on every word of God [cf. Deut 8:3; Matt 4:4]. Drink this word, but drink it in order. First drink in the Old Testament; quickly bring yourself also to drink in the New Testament.[9]

About the time of the death of Origen was born the man who would become the father of Christian monasticism, Anthony of Egypt. Athanasius tells how Anthony heard the word of God read in church, specifically Christ's invitation to the disciple to sell all he possessed and follow him. Anthony responded by selling his possessions, taking care that his sister was provided for, and leaving the city to devote his life exclusively to the following of Christ. His withdrawal into the desert outside of Alexandria is regarded as the founding step in Christian monasticism. After studying the virtues of holy men living outside the city, Anthony struck deeper into the desert to live a solitary life. Encountering violent temptations and the attacks of demons, he learned by painful experience how to counter them with Christ. Through rigorous asceticism and constant prayer, he learned to cooperate with divine grace in overcoming the passions and growing in Christian virtue. After decades of spiritual combat, Anthony became renowned in Lower Egypt for his self-mastery and was sought out by crowds of pilgrims for prayer and advice.

With the conversion of Constantine and the Edict of Milan, many Christians streamed into the desert in imitation of Anthony. The experience of these men and women bore fruit in collections of sayings which would provide guidance for new generations seeking a life of holiness. In these early decades of monasticism, the reading of Scripture is not so much explicitly promoted as

9. Ambrose, *Enarratio in Psalmum I*, section 33 (PL 14, 983–984).

everywhere assumed. The monk is one who seeks to follow the Christ whom he knows through the Scriptures. The holy texts were memorized and constantly recited to oneself in the solitude of the cell.

Anthony and his imitators were solitaries, but already in his lifetime there arose in the desert communities of men committed to the service of Christ. The "Father" of these was Saint Pachomius, who died in 346 CE. In the regulations for the communities founded by him he prescribes, "There shall be no one whatever in the monastery who does not learn to read and does not memorize something of the Scriptures, at least the New Testament and the Psalter."[10] The reading and reciting of Scripture was to accompany every moment of the monk's life, including work (e.g., waiting on the brethren, baking bread, moving to or from the place of synaxis, etc.).[11] It was less theory than practice that led the monks to this means of attaining union with Christ. The fruit of Pachomius's own "inhabiting" of the Scriptures appears most remarkably in his catechesis of an angry monk, in which he treats a tortured soul by applying the "medicine" of appropriate texts of sacred Scripture.[12]

The *Rules* of Pachomius traveled quickly to the West via their translation by the young Saint Jerome. An ardent proponent of the monastic life, Jerome saw daily intercourse with the word of God as the heart of Christian life. He writes of the monk Bonosus alone on his island: "Confident, fearless, and armed with the Apostle, now he listens to God when he reads the divine words, now he speaks with God when he pleads with the Lord."[13] To Eustochium he writes (ca. 384): "You pray, you speak to the Spouse; you read, he speaks to you."[14] Clearly outlined is the constant succession of reading and prayer that would become the hallmark of medieval monasticism. In another letter Jerome cites the same alternation in the practice of Origen, whose disciple and patron Ambrose "never took food in the presence of Origen without reading, never went to sleep unless one of the brothers was reciting the sacred writings. This

10. *Rules of Pachomius* 140, trans. Armand Veilleux, *Pachomian Koinonia*, vol. 2 (Kalamazoo, MI: Cistercian Publications, 1981), p. 166.

11. The third successor of Pachomius, Horsiesios, writes in his *Testament*: "Let us devote ourselves to reading and learning the scriptures, reciting them continually, aware of the text, 'A man shall be filled with the fruit of his own mouth, and he will be paid the price of his labors' (Prov 13:2a, Wis 10:17a). These are the [words] which lead us to eternal life. . . . [T]he word of the Lord urges us to recite the holy Scriptures that we may possess through faith what we have repeated with our mouth." *The Testament of Horsiesios*, in *Pachomian Koinonia*, vol. 3, p. 210.

12. See *Instruction concerning a Spiteful Monk*, in *Pachomian Koinonia* 3:13–41.

13. Jerome, Letter 3, section 4 (PL 22, 334).

14. Jerome, Letter 22, section 25 (PL 22, 411).

was their habit day and night so that reading (*lectio*) would succeed prayer and prayer reading."[15]

This personal intercourse with Scripture had already been propounded in the West by Cyprian in a formulation that would frequently be echoed by monastic writers in the West: "Be assiduous either in prayer or reading: now you speak with God, now God with you."[16] For Jerome, acquaintance with the sacred text was so important that he counsels the cleric Nepotian never to let the sacred reading (*sacra lectio*) out of his hands: "Learn what you have to teach,"[17] a good counsel for seminarians. Saint Ambrose, Jerome's older contemporary, similarly declared the obligation of clerics to frequent the Scriptures: "Why not employ those periods when you are free from church responsibilities in reading? Why not go to see Christ again, speak to Christ, listen to Christ? We speak to him when we pray, we listen to him when we read the divine oracles."[18]

Athanasius's *Life of Anthony*, written in 357, the year after Anthony's death, was quickly translated into Latin and created a sensation in the West, not least in the life of Saint Augustine. But the chief exponent of eremitical life, as opposed to the cenobitic monasticism of Pachomius, was John Cassian, a Scythian by birth who spent sixteen years in the Egyptian desert visiting and learning from the solitaries there. At the end of the fourth century, he moved to Marseilles and devoted the rest of his life to writing his twelve books of *Institutes* and twenty-four books of *Conferences* that were to constitute the primary source for the great Western monastic rule, the Rule of Benedict. In the *Institutes* he described the external observances of the Egyptian cenobites (Books I–IV) and their teaching on the discernment of the principal vices against which the monk must take arms (Books V–XII). The *Conferences* developed the higher dimensions of the spiritual life. While in Egypt, Cassian became the disciple of a monk who had been educated in Athens, Evagrius of Pontus. It was this figure who brought his understanding of Greek philosophy to bear on the spiritual life as lived by the largely uneducated Coptic monks. Evagrius and his mentors, the Cappadocian Fathers, were able to synthesize the *praxis* of the Egyptian monks with a well-developed *theoria* of the spiritual life whose roots can be traced back to Origen. It is this form of "learned monasticism" that was expounded by Cassian.

15. Jerome, Letter 43, section 1 (PL 22, 478).

16. Cyprian, Letter to Donatus 1, section 15 (PL 4, 226).

17. Jerome, Letter 52, section 7 (PL 22, 533).

18. Ambrose, *De Officiis*, trans. Ivor J. Davidson (New York: Oxford University Press, 2001), book 1, section 88, p. 169.

The works of Cassian became a rich source of spiritual and ascetical theology in the West. Fifty years after his death was born Saint Benedict, who would come to write a Rule for monks drawing on the teaching of John Cassian, Pachomius, Basil, Augustine, and other monastic sources. For our purposes the relevant chapter of the Rule is Chapter 48, "On the Daily Manual Labor."[19] Having in earlier chapters laid out the role of the abbot in the community and the monk's duty of obedience, Benedict proceeds to the external observances of the monastery, chief of which is the *opus Dei* or chanting of the divine office. After detailed prescriptions for the liturgy, he legislates for the rest of the monks' daily occupations. These are two: manual labor and *lectio divina*. The monks should work for their daily bread as well as allow generous time for reading the Scriptures. In summer they spend two hours of the middle of the day in reading; in winter they read for two hours in the morning and again after the completion of work. Benedict says little more about this daily reading. For beginners it would consist of memorizing psalms, for others deepening familiarity with the various books.

The Rule of Benedict was one among thirty Latin monastic rules[20]; little is known about its observance before the age of Charlemagne, when it established itself as the principal rule in the West. For the early Middle Ages, one gains some idea of the practice of *lectio* from Pope Gregory the Great (d. 610). He writes to the emperor's physician,

> What is sacred Scripture but a kind of letter of the omnipotent God to his creature? . . . The emperor of heaven, Lord of men and angels, has transmitted to you his own letters for the benefit of your life. . . . Study, therefore, I beg you, and daily meditate on the words of your creator. *Learn the heart of God in the words of God,* so that you may more ardently long for things eternal, so that your mind might be enkindled with greater desire for the joys of heaven. The more restless you are now in your love for your maker, the more rest you will have then.[21]

It is worth noting that this recommendation is made not to monks or clerics but to a highly placed layman.

A commentary on the Rule of Benedict written more than two centuries

19. See Timothy Fry et al., eds., *RB 1980: The Rule of Saint Benedict in Latin and English with Notes* (Collegeville, MN: Liturgical Press, 1981).

20. While the Latin rules prescribe times for *lectio,* few express its purpose as concisely as the Rule of Ferréol, which declares that from Scripture one "drinks salvation." *Rule of Ferréol* 19 (PL 66, 966a).

21. Gregory, *Letters,* book 4, letter 31 (PL 77, 706b); emphasis mine.

later by Smaragdus of Saint-Mihiel spells out in detail the fruits of reading combined with prayer:

> For those who practice it, the experience of *lectio sacra* sharpens perception, enriches understanding, rouses from sloth, banishes idleness, orders life, corrects bad habits, produces salutary weeping and draws tears from contrite hearts . . . curbs idle speech and vanity, awakens longing for Christ and the heavenly homeland. It must always be accompanied by prayer and intimately joined with it, for we are cleansed by prayer and taught by reading. Therefore, whoever wishes to be with God at all times must pray often and read often, for when we pray it is we who speak with God, but when we read it is God who speaks with us. Every seeker of perfection advances in reading, prayer and meditation. Reading enables us to learn what we do not know, meditation enables us to retain what we have learned, and prayer enables us to live what we have retained. Reading Sacred Scripture confers on us two gifts: it makes the soul's understanding keener, and after snatching us from the world's vanities, it leads us to the love of God.[22]

It will be noted that Smaragdus adds to the traditional pair *lectio-oratio* a third step, that of meditation. Already for Origen, the reading of the word of God had to be followed by an assiduous reflection if one were to extract the spiritual marrow of the passage.[23] The speaking to God that followed the listening would include both meditative inquiry and ardent petition for the enlightenment of the Spirit, since "most necessary for understanding the things of God is prayer."[24] To the three activities mentioned by Smaragdus—reading, meditation, prayer—would eventually be added a fourth, that of contemplation. The Carthusian Prior Guigo II at the end of the twelfth century would give the classic formulation of the stages of monastic *lectio divina*: *lectio, meditatio, oratio, contemplatio.*

Guigo gives several concise descriptions of the four stages.

> Reading seeks for the sweetness of a blessed life, meditation perceives it, prayer asks for it, contemplation tastes it. Reading, as it were, puts food whole into the mouth, meditation chews it and breaks it up, prayer

22. Smaragdus of Saint-Mihiel, *Comm. in Reg. S. Benedicti,* ad cap. 4, n. 56, cited in Mariano Magrassi, *Praying the Bible: An Introduction to Lectio Divina* (Collegeville, MN: Liturgical Press, 1998), 20.

23. Jerome says the "marrow of the Spirit" is contained in Scripture; *In Amos,* book 2, chapter 5 (PL 25, 1086b). For Gregory "within the letter is hidden the spiritual marrow." *Homilies on Ezekiel,* book 2, homily 10, section 2 (PL 76, 1058). See Ignace de la Potterie, "The Spiritual Sense of Scripture," *Communio* 23, no. 4 (Winter 1996): 738–756, at 753.

24. Origen, *Letter to Gregory Thaumaturgus* 3 (PG 11, 92).

> extracts its flavor, contemplation is the sweetness itself which gladdens and refreshes.[25]

Meditation is analogous to the rumination by which certain animals digest their food.[26]

> Reading works on the outside, meditation on the pith; prayer asks for what we long for, contemplation gives us delight in the sweetness which we have found.[27]

The twelfth century was the golden age of monastic theology, a theology completely grounded in the loving exploration of sacred Scripture. The newly founded Cistercians rediscovered the works of the Greek Fathers. Here is Gilbert of Hoyland, who continued Bernard's unfinished commentary on the Song of Songs, writing of the Christian's intimate interaction with the scriptural word: "Hold fast what you hold, and touch lingeringly and lovingly the word of life. Unroll the scroll of life, the scroll which Jesus unrolls or rather which is Jesus himself. Wrap yourself in him. . . . Put on your Beloved, our Lord

25. Guigo II, *Ladder of Monks* 3, trans. Edmund Colledge and James Walsh, *The Ladder of Monks and Twelve Meditations* (Garden City, NY: Doubleday, 1978), pp. 82–83. For a more thorough treatment of Guigo II's contribution to *lectio divina*, see Daniel Keating, "*Oratio* and *Contemplatio* (and *Actio*) of *Lectio Divina*," 98–110, at 99–102 of the present volume.

26. Rufinus reports of Didymus the Blind: "When the reader fell asleep for weariness, Didymus did not repose, but as it were chewed the cud of what he had heard until he seemed to have inscribed it on the pages of his mind." Cited in John Chapman, "Didymus the Blind," in *The Catholic Encyclopedia*, vol. 4 (New York: Robert Appleton Company, 1908), 784. See also Cassian: Ita fiet ut non solum omnis directio ac meditatio cordis tui, verum etiam cunctae evagationes atque discursus cogitationum tuarum sint tibi divinae legis sancta et incessabilis ruminatio. ("It will come about that not only every movement and meditation of your heart but also all the meanderings and ponderings of your thoughts become for you the holy and continual rumination of the divine law.") *Conference* 14, chapter 13 (PL 49, 981). Mario Masini gives a full description: "In reference to the word of God, *ruminatio* assumes meanings more and more defined by its nuances: to repeat the word that has been heard in a way that it presents itself to the reader in all its concreteness . . . , to return to the meaning of the word in order to enter into the depths of its message, to repeat the word or its essential message in a concise expression so as to be able 'to savor' it, to allow the message to descend from the mind which understood it to the 'heart,' the place which it recognizes as its own proper abode. The profound meaning of *ruminatio* is clarified by St. Caesarius of Arles (6th century) when he explains that it is an 'intimate penetration, under the guidance of grace, of the profound wonders of the word of God.' The spiritual dimension of *ruminatio* is made explicit by St. Gregory the Great's teaching that it serves to 'open the way for the Lord so that He can enter into our hearts and inflame them with the grace of His love.'" *Lectio Divina: An Ancient Prayer That Is Ever New*, trans. Edmund C. Lane (New York: Alba House, 1998), 85.

27. Guigo II, *Ladder of Monks* 3, p. 83.

Jesus Christ . . . for his word is a flame. Herein repose."[28] The metaphors tumble out as the writer strives to capture the monk's engagement with the Word. For Godfrey of Admont (d. 1165), sacred Scripture is "the breast of Jesus."[29] William of Firmat (d. ca. 1095) echoes the Song of Songs: "I have scarcely begun to read the text and already I have found him whom I love."[30]

By the end of the twelfth century a new approach to theology was gaining ground. New sciences were developing, the writings of Aristotle were rediscovered, a need was felt for a more systematic organization and study of Christian knowledge. According to Beryl Smalley, "The innumerable problems arising from the reception of Aristotelian logic and the study of canon and civil law, the new possibilities of reasoning, the urgent need for speculation and discussion, all these produced an atmosphere of haste and excitement which was unfavourable to biblical scholarship."[31]

The new scholasticism

> marks the great watershed in the evolution of Christian thought between the "wisdom" of the Fathers and the "science" of modern theology. Study is concerned with scientific certitude; *lectio* wishes to nourish a spiritual experience. Study takes place on the objective and detached level of investigation; *lectio* takes place in the contemplative atmosphere of prayer. Professional exegetes strive to prescind from personal feelings. Spiritual persons approach the Bible like Bernard, with open mouth and heart. Fervent before they start to read, they read in order to become even more fervent. Their aim is not to construct a science, but wisdom, which is contemplative knowledge. They do not proceed by way of a specific analytic technique, but trust the intuitions of their grace-filled soul.[32]

28. Magrassi, *Praying the Bible*, 52–53.

29. Magrassi, *Praying the Bible*, 55.

30. William of Firmat, *Exhortation*, cited in Mariano Magrassi, "Lectio Divina," in *Dizionario enciclopedico de spiritualità*, ed. Ermanno Ancilli and the Pontificio Istituto di Spiritualità, vol. 2 (Rome: Città Nuova Editrice, 1990), p. 1412.

31. Beryl Smalley, *The Study of the Bible in the Middle Ages* (South Bend, IN: University of Notre Dame Press, 1978), 77.

32. Magrassi, *Praying the Bible*, 73–74. In the late thirteenth century Roger Bacon would lament, "Although the principal preoccupation of theologians in their studies ought to have been a concern with their own text, it should be acknowledged . . . that for fifty years they have been mainly occupied with questions. This has been made plain and evident to everybody through their tracts and summas and the huge, ponderous works written by many of them, although it must be said that these do not deal with God's most sacred text. For this reason, it is clear that theologians are more inclined to deal with questions rather than the text." Cited in Henri de Lubac, *Medieval Exegesis: The Four Senses of Scripture*, vol. 1, trans. Mark Sebanc (Grand Rapids: Eerdmans, 1998), 72.

While such a demarcation between the two approaches can be overdrawn, particularly if one remembers the devotion of Thomas Aquinas to the "sacred page," it is nonetheless true that theology after the twelfth century shifted its attention to rational analysis and systematization. The great scholastics of the thirteenth century continued to conceive of logical argument as developing the truths of Scripture, but the method bore in it the seeds of a neglect of the sacred text. Yves Congar speaks of "the danger of developing theology in a purely dialectical and deductive manner, using the biblical texts in an accidental manner simply for decorative purposes."[33]

Systematic theology, a necessary development for the rational analysis of the faith, entailed a departure from the interior, affective theology of the patristic and monastic Fathers.

> If one were to characterize the *lectio* of the [scholastic] master . . . one could say that it was before anything else an exegesis; i.e., an interpretation attempting to explore the objective substance of a text, whatever the subjective needs or the results obtained. . . . The word of God was treated as an "object," given, to be certain, within the context of the faith, but apart from one's own fervor and experience.[34]

The loss of the affective element was compensated for by the rise of new forms of devotion that would culminate in the *devotio moderna* of the fourteenth century. The reading of Scripture became one of several methods for developing an interior life. Greater attention was paid to the psychological states of the praying individual. Thinkers of the mendicant orders tended to use Scripture texts as props for intellectual arguments or to teach moral and ascetic lessons rather than as an entry into contemplation. The reading of other spiritual writers was put on the same level as Scripture.[35] In the sixteenth century the Jesu-

33. Yves Congar, *The History of Theology*, trans. Hunter Guthrie (Garden City, NY: Doubleday, 1968), 140. I am grateful to Professor Lawrence Welch for drawing my attention to this assessment.

34. Marie-Dominique Chenu, *Nature, Man, and Society in the Twelfth Century: Essays on New Theological Perspectives in the Latin West*, cited in Raymond Studzinski, *Reading To Live: The Evolving Practice of Lectio Divina* (Collegeville, MN: Liturgical Press, 2009), 172.

35. "In sum, in *lectio divina* the centralizing element in the contemplative process was the biblical text itself. This was the constant reference point for the author's reflections and therefore for his or her conception of literary identity. In *lectio spiritualis* the centralizing element was the thinking subject, who was the source of the continuity of the contemplative process and therefore the source of literary identity. One sign of this emphasis appears in authors who mentioned among their recommendations the reading of edifying works other than the Bible. . . . This period of consolidation in the history of *lectio spiritualis* runs roughly from the founding of the Devotio Moderna in the fourteenth century to the high spirituality of Francois de Sales,

its would advocate not *lectio divina* but "spiritual reading,"[36] which included the devotional reading of spiritual masters. "The new method," writes Charles Dumont, "was to bear other fruit, but the personal contact of heart and mind with the Holy Scripture would lose its character of direct encounter with the Word, with Incarnate Wisdom."[37]

Only in modern times has the Church rediscovered the richness of the word of God as a privileged means of knowing God and developing friendship with him. One may cite three towering figures at the turn of the twentieth century: Saint Thérèse of Lisieux, Saint Elizabeth of the Trinity, and Blessed Columba Marmion. The young Saint Thérèse opened the New Testament and found there the answer to all her spiritual questions.[38] Book Three alone of her autobiography contains references to Proverbs, Isaiah, the Last Supper Discourse, the High Priestly Prayer, other discourses in the Gospel of John, the Sermon on the Mount, the Psalms, the Letters to the Romans and Corinthians, the Song of Songs, and stories of Jesus in the Gospel of Luke. Her reflections on these passages breathe the excitement of new discovery that reminds one of Rupert of Deutz, Saint Bernard, the Victorines, and the other medievals. Saint Elizabeth of the Trinity a decade later found a vibrant accord between

who died in 1622." Brian Stock, *After Augustine: The Meditative Reader and the Text* (Philadelphia: University of Pennsylvania Press, 2001), 107–108.

36. "In this new 'spiritual reading' the text assumed a subordinate role. It is the affective life of the reader that becomes more important. His or her emotional experience in the reading of a particular text moves into prominence. In other words, the text is no longer central; the person of the reader as a thinking and feeling subject is. This focus would prevail after the fourteenth century. Lost was the vital direct contact with the word that was at the center of the ancients' approach to reading." Studzinski, *Reading to Live*, 173–174.

37. Charles Dumont, *Praying the Word of God* (Oxford: SLG Press, 1999), 15.

38. "I decided to consult St. Paul's epistles in the hopes of getting an answer. It was the twelfth and thirteenth chapters of First Corinthians that claimed my attention." *Autobiography*, trans. Ronald Knox (New York: P. J. Kenedy & Sons, 1958), 234. "I looked in the Bible for some hint about the lift I wanted, and I came across the passage where Eternal Wisdom says: 'Is anyone simple as a little child? Then let him come to me' (Prov 9:4). To that Wisdom I went. . . . I read on, and this is what I found: 'I will console you like a mother caressing her son; you shall be like children carried at the breast fondled on a mother's lap' (Isa 66:12–13). Never were words so touching: never was such music to rejoice the heart" (248–249). "Doesn't St. Paul tell us that we can't even say 'Father' to our Father in heaven without the aid of his loving Spirit (Rom 8:15)? Surely, then he can make use of me" (278). "He let me into the meaning of that phrase in the Canticles, 'Draw me . . . we hasten!' (Song 1:3)" (305). "You've said to me what the father said to the Prodigal Son in the parable: 'Everything that I have already is thine' (Luke 15:31); and as these are your words [the priestly prayer of John 17], dear Jesus, they belong to me" (308). "One glance at the holy Gospel and the life of Jesus becomes a perfume that fills the very air I breathe; I know at once which way to run" (311).

the New Testament and the writings of Ruysbroeck and John of the Cross. The first page of her first spiritual treatise, "Heaven in Faith," contains references to John 17, 8, and 15, Isaiah 45, Romans 6, Ephesians 2, Hosea 2, Philippians 3, Psalm 41, and Revelation 14—all woven seamlessly into her own spiritual insight and quotation from the mystics.[39] Blessed Columba Marmion in the opening decades of the century expounded carefully the beauty of divine adoptive sonship as presented in the Scriptures and expressed in the liturgy of the Church. This rediscovery of Scripture as a lifeline to God in the contemporary world found full expression in the magisterium of the Church at the Second Vatican Council. Paragraph 25 of *Dei verbum* commends the regular reading of sacred Scripture to all Christians as the privileged means of growing in union with Christ.[40] Finally, with *Verbum Domini* the encouragement of *lectio divina* for priests, seminarians, laypeople, and consecrated faithful has come fully into its own.[41]

Characteristics of *Lectio Divina*

We have defined *lectio* as a personal encounter with the risen Christ through reading of the inspired word. The many dimensions of this encounter are suggested by some modern descriptions:

- Louis Bouyer: "A personal reading of the Word of God during which we try to assimilate its substance; a reading in faith, in a spirit of prayer, believing in the real presence of God who speaks to us in the sacred text, while

39. Elizabeth of the Trinity, *I Have Found God: Complete Works*, vol. 1, trans. Alethia Kane (Washington, DC: ICS Publications, 1984), 94.

40. "Therefore, all the clergy must hold fast to the Sacred Scriptures through diligent sacred reading and careful study, especially the priests of Christ and others, such as deacons and catechists who are legitimately active in the ministry of the word. This is to be done so that none of them will become 'an empty preacher of the word of God outwardly, who is not a listener to it inwardly' since they must share the abundant wealth of the divine word with the faithful committed to them, especially in the sacred liturgy. The sacred synod also earnestly and especially urges all the Christian faithful, especially Religious, to learn by frequent reading of the divine Scriptures the 'excellent knowledge of Jesus Christ' (Phil. 3:8). 'For ignorance of the Scriptures is ignorance of Christ' . . . And let them remember that prayer should accompany the reading of Sacred Scripture, so that God and man may talk together; for 'we speak to Him when we pray; we hear Him when we read the divine sayings.'" Second Vatican Council, *Dei verbum* (November 18, 1965), 111–128 in *The Documents of Vatican II*, trans. Joseph Gallagher, ed. Walter M. Abbot (New York: Guild Press, 1966), §25, p. 127.

41. See Pope Benedict XVI, *Verbum Domini*, §80–84, §86–87.

the monk himself strives to be present in a spirit of obedience and total surrender to the divine promises and demands."[42]

- CHARLES DUMONT: "The free and existential use of Scripture by the praying soul."[43]
- BLESSED COLUMBA MARMION: "Reading under the eye of God until the heart is touched and leaps to flame."[44]
- MARIANO MAGRASSI: "Diligent reading fed by hunger based on love—savory knowledge tasted in inner experience—dialogue with the living God that breaks into prayer upon receiving a living and personal Word . . . total submission to the word."[45]
- C. JEAN-NESMY: "An astonishing, contemplative reading in which the Word of God reveals to each one, personally, how his own special vocation fits into the convergence of all, towards the one salvation in Christ."[46]

While a loving conversation does not lend itself to scientific analysis, these existential descriptions enable us to identify some salient features of Christian *lectio.*

Lectio is first of all an *affective* reading. It engages the whole person, mind and heart, soul and body. For Gregory the Great, the divine words are addressed to the heart.[47] Even the lips are involved as one recites to oneself the sacred text. For Aelred of Rievaulx the sacred text was a source of consolation and joy:

> Truly, my brothers, when inner disquiet or cares cast us down, we find in the Holy Scriptures the consolation we need. "For indeed, all that has been written was written for our learning, in order that the consolation of the Scriptures might bring us hope." (Rom. 15:4) I assure you, no adversity can befall us, no sadness, no bitterness that does not, as soon as the sacred text is revealed to us, quickly disappear, or become bearable. This is the field where Isaac went to meditate as the day waned, and Rebecca coming to meet him, soothed by her gentleness the pain that had seized him. (Gen. 24:64) How often, Jesus, the day wanes and night comes on, how often all becomes distasteful and everything I see is a burden to me. If someone

42. *Parola, Chiesa e Sacramenti nel Protestantesimo e nel Cattolicesimo,* cited in Magrassi, *Praying the Bible,* 18.

43. Charles Dumont, *Praying the Word of God,* 25.

44. Frequently cited without a reference, as in Thelma Hall, *Too Deep for Words: Rediscovering Lectio Divina* (New York: Paulist, 1988), 44.

45. Magrassi, *Praying the Bible,* 84–85.

46. Cited in Masini, *Lectio Divina: An Ancient Prayer That Is Ever New,* 27–28.

47. Gregory, *In Ezechielem,* book 1, homily 1, sections 1 and 15; book 1, homily 6, sections 16–17 (PL 76, 787ab, 793ab, 836b, 837a).

> speaks, I hardly hear them. My heart becomes as hard as a stone. What am I to do at such times? I go out to meditate in the field, I open the sacred book, I read and engrave my thoughts on this wax: and suddenly, Rebecca, that is, your grace, Lord, comes towards me, her light scatters my darkness, drives away my cares, breaks my hardness. How much to be pitied are those who, troubled by sadness, do not enter into that field and find joy.[48]

If *lectio* is affective, it is because it is the encounter with a person, with God the divine author and with his Son Christ the Word, the Logos who "becomes accessible only in his historic incarnation, from which are inseparable all these human words of the Old and New Testament, in which and through which the eternal Word has come close to us and saved us."[49] For Gaudentius of Brescia (d. 410)

> the whole body of divine Scripture, both the Old and the New Testament, contains the Son of God: either promising that he will come among men or declaring that he has already come. Wherefore blessed Philip, when he was found by Christ, found Nathanael and said to him: "We have found the one of whom Moses wrote in the Law and the Prophets, Jesus, son of Joseph from Nazareth." What is more, dearest ones, in him is contained the whole Law both new and old, and he himself is, as it were, the soul of the Law.[50]

48. Cited in Dumont, *Praying the Word of God*, 17.

49. Louis Bouyer and L. Dattrino, *La Spiritualità dei Padri* 3/A, cited in Guido Bendinelli [and others], *Parola di Dio: S. Scrittura e tradizione nei Padri dei primi secoli*, DSBP 47 (Rome: Borla, 2008), 216.

50. *Second Discourse on Exodus* (PL 20, 856a). Hilary sees Christ acting already in the patriarchs: "It is he who through the whole extent of the present age, through true and manifest adumbrations, generates, cleanses, sanctifies, chooses, separates, or redeems the Church in the Patriarchs, through Adam's slumber, Noah's flood, Melchizedek's blessing, Abraham's justification, Isaac's birth, and Jacob's bondage." *Treatise on the Mysteries*, book 1, preface (SC 19B), pp. 73–75. See also de Lubac: "Jesus Christ brings about the unity of Scripture, because he is the endpoint and fullness of Scripture. Everything in it is related to him. In the end he is its sole object. Consequently, he is, so to speak, its whole exegesis. . . . Cornerstone that he is, he joins together the two Testaments, just as he joins together the two peoples. He is the Head of the body of the Scriptures, just as he is the Head of the body of His Church. He is the Head of all sacred understanding, just as he is the head of all the elect. He is the whole content of Scripture, just as he contains all of it in him." *Medieval Exegesis*, 1:237. Paschasius Radbertus declared the two Testaments to be of one heart and one mind in the unity of Christ: "Unanimes in unitate Christi inveniuntur—Christus ipse eorum consensus est." *In Matthaeum*, book 8, chapter 18 (PL 120, 623c, 624d). For Gilbert of Hoyland, "the essential task of exegesis . . . is to apply everything to the mystery of Christ." *In Cantica*, sermon 30, section 5 (PL 184, 157c), in Magrassi, *Praying the Bible*, 44. "The Christian understanding throughout history has been that '*Christus in littera continetur*': and so 'Scripture as a whole is a great "sacrament" which contains, in a sort of material husk, the mystery of salvation whose center is Christ. Guided by the Spirit, I must

Sacred reading is *relational*, a listening to the risen Lord speaking to us now through these sacred words.[51] He is the one who loves me, who knows me intimately, who loves parts of me I may not even be aware of yet or that I have hidden from him.[52] He tells me what he wants to be for me, the secrets of his heart, what he wants to do in my life. My task is to listen, to receive, like Mary. One reads the text slowly, more than once, recalling that every word of the Lord, even the most challenging, is a word of love for me personally, the love shown in the sacrifice of Christ on the cross. How is God revealing to me his love in Christ through this particular text, whether the New or the Old Testament?

As I listen to the word I experience the third element of *lectio*, its *transforming* power. If the Lord speaks to me in the text, I lay myself open to his saving power, his healing. I receive like good soil the gifts he offers, allowing him to transform me slowly into his own self.[53] After I reflect on what I hear the Lord saying to me, my spirit will inevitably break into prayer, asking the Lord to perfect in me that which he is giving me, asking for the power to live out in daily life the beauty of his Gospel. I become aware that Christian life,

enter through the 'letter' and keep going into the depths of mystery, where I meet him." Mariano Magrassi, "Bibbia Pregata," in *L'"oggi" della Parola di Dio nella liturgia* (Torino-Leumann: Elledici, 1970), 212.

51. "[T]he act of listening to Scripture becomes an experience of the present Lord." Enzo Bianchi, *Lectio Divina: From God's Word to Our Lives* (Brewster, MA: Paraclete Press, 2015), 70.

52. Kierkegaard calls Scripture a "love-letter" from God to the individual: "The Bible is for the solitary. Imagine a couple who love one another. The lover has written a letter to the beloved; now, would it ever occur to the recipient to worry about how other people would understand it? Would she not read it on her own? Let us suppose now that the love-letter in question was peculiar in this respect, that it was addressed to every single human being as the beloved, then what? What sense would it make for all those solitary beings to be there conferring together, let alone loading themselves with a whole baggage of erudition inherited from countless generations!

"No, the intention of that letter is that each one should read it before God and in solitude, like someone who has received it as a personal gift from God." Cited in Dumont, *Praying the Word*, 19.

53. "For Origen, at the heart of biblical interpretation was not its grammatico-historical understanding but the sacramental presence of the Logos in Scripture, which is powerfully effective to transform its hearers into the image of God. The word of God is living and active to breathe new life. A proper response to this great mystery is not merely through historical-critical scholarship but through prayerful participation in the sacrament of God's word." Shin, "Some Light from Origen," 414–415. See also Magrassi's summary of the teaching of Cassian: "The Word of God molds the secret depths of our soul, becomes part of our inner world, seeps into our mind as if by osmosis. . . . [A] time would come when continuous meditation would impregnate your soul and mold it in his image." *Praying the Bible*, 69.

obedience to the law of Christ, is not my own achievement but the work of the Spirit[54] in me, a work which I can only implore as a mendicant. I will ask for cleansing from my sin, allowing myself to feel the Word as a purifying fire.[55] At the same time my spirit will respond to the Lord's graciousness with praise and thanksgiving with all the affection of my heart. The transformative power of *lectio* will be shown in daily life in my growing ability to carry out the commandments of Jesus, in particular the new commandment of fraternal love. In the parable of Jesus, the word of God received in a "noble and generous heart" brings forth a harvest of good works (cf. Luke 8:15 NJB). For this reason Pope Benedict added a fifth step to the traditional four steps of *lectio*, namely the step of action.[56] The fruit of hearing is love in action.[57]

A final dimension of *lectio divina* can be called *ecclesial*: it builds one onto sacred history. As we take in the story of God's deeds for his people and his generous love, we find ourselves slowly being built onto the Church, onto the foundation of all those who have believed in Christ and been made part of his people. Jean Leclercq writes,

> There is a unity among all the successive phases of the divine economy; in the period of the Old Testament as in every epoch of the Church, there is enacted one history of salvation which has found its completion in the paschal mystery, but in which every Christian, every monk must participate, which he should in some way relive, renew in himself—something not possible if he has not made his own the mysteries spoken of in the Sacred Scriptures which have recounted this history. In a certain way the same Spirit

54. For Saint Jerome reading "opens the sails" to the Spirit. *In Ezechielem*, book 12, preface (PL 25, 369d).

55. "The Word must wound. In other words, it must challenge false situations, give rise to second thoughts, create *metanoia*. If the Word grazes the outer layer of the soul without wounding our thoughts, heart and life, reading becomes formalism. The Word which proceeds from God's innermost life wishes to lay hold of ours, to reach the depths of our being, the 'marrow.' The prophets described this realistically: 'Son of man, eat this scroll.' Eating is the act that seals Ezekiel's vocation. Jeremiah, too, feels the Word like a burning fire shut up in his bones (20:9). It is like lava that explodes from a volcano and forcefully creates a channel: 'I am weary holding it in, and I cannot.'" Magrassi, *Praying the Bible*, 100–101.

56. See Bianchi, *Lectio*, 71.

57. "Inspired Scripture also inspires. It shows its power by making holiness blossom in the reader and bear fruit. Those who make room in themselves for the word to deploy fully its life-giving power will eventually bear witness to that power by giving their lives (*martyria*). The martyr is the quintessential 'pneumatofore' or Spirit-bearer, and in the Bible, he or she confesses with undeniable force both the inspired quality of Scripture and the way that it inspires." Bianchi, *Lectio*, 71.

> of God which inspired the authors of the Sacred Books continues to act in those who read it, who seek to experience the reality of which they speak.[58]

We continue sacred history.[59] The grace that circulates in the Church comes to draw us into the mystery of the Body of Christ. We learn to receive that love, to find our place in the Body, and to hand on that love in ever more authentic ways. The reading of Scripture becomes less mastery of a subject than entrance into a life, the life of the Son of God.[60]

Seminary Formation in *Lectio*

If *lectio divina* is a daily personal encounter with the risen Christ, how can we promote its practice in seminary formation? This we need to do if we are to take *Verbum Domini* seriously. Since it is only recently that the tradition of *lectio* is being promoted in seminaries, this part of the paper can only offer some observations and suggestions.

In what follows, I will provide an overview of some of the ways *lectio divina* has been fostered in the seminary I am familiar with, Kenrick-Glennon Seminary in St. Louis, Missouri. At our seminary there is no formal introduction to *lectio divina*, but a group *lectio* is practiced once a week. The seminarians assemble in one of the chapels; the Gospel for the following Sunday is read aloud once, then after several minutes' pause, a second time. Generous quiet time follows during which the men listen in their minds and hearts to what the Lord might be saying to them in the passage. Finally, those seminarians who wish come to the microphone and share what they heard addressed to them in the readings. The period begins with prayer and a short hymn and ends with prayer, the whole lasting 45 minutes.

58. Jean Leclercq, "Lectio Divina," 562–566 in *Dizionario degli Istituti di Perfezione*, vol. 5, ed. Guerrino Pelliccia and Rocca Giancarlo (Rome: Edizione Paoline, 1978), at 563.

59. See the expressive page of de Lubac alluding to numerous medieval commentators: "With Abraham we abandon our home and we arrive at the oak of Mamre, where God goes to visit us. With the children of Israel we flee 'the furnace of Egyptian servitude,' we cross the Red Sea, we wander in the desert, our forces are refreshed by a miraculous nourishment, we enter at last into the promised land. . . . Finally, whatever page I meditate upon, I find in it a means that God offers me, right now, to restore the divine image within me. Thus I myself become Jerusalem, the holy city; I become or become again the temple of the Lord; for me the promise is realized: 'I shall dwell in their midst.' God walks with me in the garden when I read the divine Scriptures." *Medieval Exegesis*, 2:141.

60. A full yet concise presentation of the major features of *lectio* is given by the Manquehue Apostolic Movement, a Private Association of Lay Faithful in Santiago, Chile, whose spirituality is centered on monastic *lectio divina*. See www.manquehue.org/mam/lectio-divina/que-es/.

At the beginning of the year the students are given a booklet summarizing some steps in *lectio*. The booklet is titled *WRAP Yourself in Scripture*, by Karen L. Dwyer and Lawrence A. Dwyer, and is published by the Institute for Priestly Formation. "WRAP" is an acronym for the steps recommended in this method: Write, Reflect, Apply, and Praise. One uses a journal to write out the text of the *lectio* reading and record thoughts one has about the readings. The method is influenced by Ignatian prayer, and the men are free to avail themselves of it if they wish.

New Testament professor Randy Soto has drawn up another aid which he makes available to his students. His method breaks down into practical steps the five movements described by Pope Benedict. He introduces the method in a short booklet titled *Lectio Divina: Praying with the Word of God* and published by Vox Christi Publishing.[61]

The seminarians are encouraged to practice *lectio* daily, and it is clear from their conversation about prayer that they are beginning to internalize the practice. Those who preach begin their homily preparation with *lectio*. However, it seems important for priests also to read whole texts of Scripture on their own and not just those that appear in the lectionary. In homily preparation one thinks mainly of what the text might be saying to this congregation, whereas in *lectio* one is listening to what the Lord is saying to oneself. The more the priest is permeated by the Word in his own life, the more convincingly will he be able to deliver it to others. The United States bishops have recommended *lectio divina* as a means to enable preachers to "see the world through biblical eyes."[62]

How much can *lectio* be taught in the Scripture class? One New Testament professor at Kenrick-Glennon Seminary gives several *lectio* assignments each semester. Apart from direct assignments the professor can always indicate how a Scripture passage has been heard in the Church and therefore how one might hear it as a member of the Church. After looking at the literal meaning of Moses' striking water from the rock, one can look at the three spiritual meanings: as an allegory of the Church being born from the side of Christ, as a metaphor for tears being struck from a hardened heart (tropology), or a type of the river of life flowing from the throne of God in the New Jerusalem (anagogy).[63]

61. Randy a Jesu Soto, *Lectio Divina: Praying with the Word of God*. (St. Louis: Vox Christi, 2013).

62. United States Conference of Catholic Bishops, *Preaching the Mystery of Faith: The Sunday Homily* (Washington, DC: United States Conference of Catholic Bishops, 2012), p. 34.

63. For the intrinsic unity of the literal and spiritual sense see de Lubac, *Medieval Exegesis*: "[I]n Scripture . . . there is no dissociation of the two senses. The spirit does not exist without the letter, nor is the letter devoid of the spirit. Each of the two senses is in the other. . . . Each

The Scripture professor needs to introduce seminarians to the many aspects under which a given text may be studied. A partial list of aspects under which an Old Testament text can be studied includes: literal meaning, historical origin, literary features, relation to other passages in same book, relation to other Old Testament passages, relation to Ancient Near East literature, relation to New Testament / Christ (typology), patristic interpretation, reception history (art, literature, music, film), and use in liturgy, theology, spirituality, papal documents, catechism, and homiletics.

The professor of spiritual theology teaches a comprehensive unit on *lectio divina*, relying primarily on the magisterial doctoral thesis of Mario Masini.[64] The homiletics professor stipulates that homily preparation begins with *lectio*. *Lectio* is a topic raised in a man's conversations with his spiritual director and his formation advisor. The weekly spiritual conference by the rector or other administrator or faculty member would provide an opportunity for guidance in *lectio*, although I understand that the topic has not been so far explicitly covered (as of spring 2017) in this context. While the seminary believes in the importance of the practice of *lectio* in the life of a priest, there is not yet a formal guidance in the practice, and several men express an uncertainty of how to go about it. A questionnaire on the practice of *lectio* given to this year's

needs the other. . . . [F]rom the start they even constitute really only one. The spiritual sense is also necessary for the completion of the literal sense, which latter is indispensable for founding it; it is therefore the natural term of divine inspiration, and, as Bossuet will say, 'pertains to the original, principal plan of the Holy Spirit.' *Christus in littera continetur. The spirit is not outside the history.* They are given together, inseparably, through the fact of a single inspiration." *Medieval Exegesis*, 2:26. For the threefold spiritual sense, see the concise summary of Nicholas of Lyra (d. 1349): "The mystic or spiritual sense . . . is in general threefold; since if the things signified by the words are referred to so as to signify the things that are to be believed in the new law, this amounts to the allegorical sense; if they are referred to so as to signify things to be done by us, this is the moral or tropological sense; and if they are referred to so as to signify things that are to be hoped for in the beatitude to come, this is the anagogical sense." Cited in de Lubac, *Medieval Exegesis*, 2:37. Aquinas gives another example of the four senses, that is, the literal and threefold spiritual senses: see de Lubac, *Medieval Exegesis*, 2:197. The four senses were expressed in the medieval hexameter couplet:

Littera gesta docet, quid credas allegoria,
Moralis quid agas, quo tendas anagogia.
The letter teaches events, allegory what you should believe.
Morality teaches what you should do, anagogy what mark you should be aiming for.

Cited in de Lubac, *Medieval Exegesis*, 1:1.

64. Mario Masini, *La "lectio divina": Teologia, spiritualità, metodo,* 2nd ed. (Milan: San Paolo, 2002). See also the shorter work based on the first edition of the thesis: *Lectio Divina*, cited above, note 26.

deacon class yielded only five out of eleven responses, of which only one could be described as enthusiastic. It would seem that *lectio divina* is here to stay in seminaries, but administrators and faculty are still trying to find their way in giving instruction about it.

The recent *Ratio Fundamentalis Institutionis Sacerdotalis* from the Congregation for the Clergy gives clear impetus for the teaching of *lectio* in seminaries:

> A relationship with the Word of God holds a preeminent place in the process of spiritual growth. Before it is ever preached the Word must be welcomed in the depth of the heart, "*above all in the context of the 'new evangelisation' to which the church is called today.*" The new evangelisation is the continuous point of reference for the life of discipleship and spiritual configuration to Christ the Good Shepherd. Seminarians need to be introduced gradually to the knowledge of the Word of God, through the method known as *Lectio Divina*. A profound daily meditation, practiced with fidelity and diligence, in which study and prayer come together in a reciprocal fruitfulness, will ensure an integral approach to both the Old and New Testaments.[65]

These instructions are a challenge and a "great door of opportunity" for us professors of the sacred word.

I will close with a citation from a doctoral thesis on the twelfth-century theologian Rupert of Deutz, written by a St. Louis priest almost fifty years ago. It suggests the relevance of monastic *lectio* for the diocesan seminarian of today. Speaking of medieval monastic writers, Eugene Selzer says they

> show us that even while theology must be true to its principles as a science, a truly living theology cannot flourish outside an atmosphere of prayer and contemplation. For them, theology was not simply a science, but a wisdom in which personal experience and love of God played a significant role. They were convinced that theology grew best through man's personal confrontation with the divine Word present in the scriptural word.[66]

Rupert's theology in particular

> is the contribution of a man whose whole life was dedicated to the study of the Scripture, of a mystic who found the Lord in gentle and intimate communion with the inspired word. . . . Every page of his writing discloses the wonder, admiration and love he felt for God and for the divine plan revealed in the sacred word.[67]

65. Congregation for the Clergy, *Ratio fundamentalis institutionis sacerdotalis* [*The Gift of the Priestly Vocation*] (December 8, 2016) (Vatican City: Libreria Editrice Vaticana), §103.

66. Eugene P. Selzer, *Rupert of Deutz: Preaching the Word of God* (Rome: Pontifical Liturgical Institute of the Pontifical Athenaeum of Saint Anselm, 1968), 67.

67. Selzer, *Rupert*, 71.

In the very different circumstances of their lives, priests of the new millennium can be animated by the same personal love and experience of the divine word.

Only a loving relationship with the risen Lord will sustain the lifelong celibacy of the priest. The encounter with this Lord in the Testaments he has given us is a privileged way of nourishing such a relationship. Our seminaries are the places where a man begins to cultivate and nurture this friendship. Teachers and formators are blessed mediators of a loving interaction with the word of God.

The Implications of Exegetical Method for *Lectio Divina*: John 6 as Treated in Three Commentaries

Michael Magee

It is a safe bet that most priests or deacons today, in their work of preparing homilies, have had the experience of opening a biblical commentary and carefully reading through its exegesis of a particular passage, only to end the exercise with no new insights to offer a congregation. This might not necessarily be because any of the material in the commentary is believed to be erroneous or unorthodox, but rather because it seems to provide little or nothing of relevance to the hearers of the divine word as they seek to apply its message to their own lives. The information contained in the commentary might actually serve to emphasize rather than to bridge the temporal divide between the writer and today's hearer of the word, or even to suggest that the text being read and proclaimed is not actually the one that the author originally intended it to be. The same priest or deacon—or any member of the faithful—might have experienced a similar aridity if he or she were utilizing the commentary as preparation for *lectio divina*, and for the same reasons.

In his address to the 14th General Congregation of the Synod of Bishops "On the Word of God in the Life and Mission of the Church," on October 14, 2008, His Holiness Pope Benedict XVI diagnosed this problem as a failure to incorporate within biblical exegesis, along with the historico-critical dimension, that aspect that he termed the "second methodological level" of exegetical work outlined in §12 of the Dogmatic Constitution on Divine Revelation of the Second Vatican Council, *Dei verbum*:

> [S]ince Holy Scripture must be read and interpreted according to the same Spirit by whom it was written, no less serious attention must be given to the content and unity of the whole of Scripture, if the meaning of the sacred texts is to be correctly brought to light. The living tradition of the whole

> Church must be taken into account along with the harmony which exists between elements of the faith. It is the task of exegetes to work according to these rules toward a better understanding and explanation of the meaning of sacred Scripture, so that through preparatory study the judgment of the Church may mature. For all of what has been said about the way of interpreting Scripture is subject finally to the judgment of the Church, which carries out the divine commission and ministry of guarding and interpreting the word of God.[1]

As Pope Benedict asserted, "The result of the absence of the *second* methodological level is what has created a profound fissure between scientific exegesis and *lectio divina*."[2]

Drawing on the same insights as further developed by the deliberations of the Synod of Bishops, Pope Benedict later outlined several troubling consequences of a "dualistic approach to sacred Scripture"; that is, one that would consist in *separating* the two methodological levels rather engaging them in their mutual reciprocity.[3] If this occurs, he states, unfortunate results may ensue, namely: 1) if the discipline of biblical exegesis itself is restricted to the first level alone, the Scriptures may be read as a book belonging only to the past; 2) the lack of a hermeneutic of faith within the exegetical task may result in its being replaced by a purely secular hermeneutic and a denial that the divine element is truly present in history; 3) the historical and biblical bases of the fundamental elements of ecclesial life may be denied, thus occasioning a sharp fissure between exegesis on the one hand, and a purely spiritualized theology devoid of real historical roots, on the other.[4]

It is important to note that Benedict certainly does not belittle the contributions of historico-critical study of sacred Scripture, which he indeed incorporates frequently into his own works. Rather, he warns against the exegete's failure to complement these contributions with the perspective of ecclesial tradition in the context of the integral deposit of faith. Perhaps too culturally specific for inclusion in an Apostolic Exhortation, but nevertheless very illustrative of the point, was Benedict's observation of the contemporary landscape

1. Second Vatican Council, *Dei verbum* (November 18, 1965), 111–128 in *The Documents of Vatican II*, trans. Joseph Gallagher, ed. Walter M. Abbot (New York: Guild Press, 1966), §12.

2. Pope Benedict XVI, Address during the 14th General Congregation of the Synod of Bishops (October 14, 2008) (emphasis added). w2.vatican.va/content/benedict-xvi/en/speeches/2008/october/documents/hf_ben-xvi_spe_20081014_sinodo.html.

3. Pope Benedict XVI, *Verbum Domini* (September 30, 2010) (Washington, DC: United States Conference of Catholic Bishops, 2010), §35.

4. Pope Benedict XVI, *Verbum Domini*, §35.

of exegesis in his native Germany, given in the above-mentioned address to the Synod:

> Today the exegetical "mainstream" in Germany, for example, denies that the Lord instituted the Holy Eucharist and says that Jesus' corpse remained in the tomb. The Resurrection in this view would not have been a historical event but a theological view. This happens because the hermeneutics of faith is missing: profane philosophical hermeneutics is affirmed instead, which deny the possibility of the entrance and presence of the Divine in history.[5]

In priestly formation, the manner in which a candidate is taught to interpret the biblical text and the resources that he learns to utilize in expounding the sacred Scriptures have implications not merely for his preparation of homilies but for his entire relationship with the sacred word. The preparation of homilies is (or at least, should be) the fruit of the priest's own prayerful assimilation of the sacred text. The centrality to his life and ministry of preaching the divine word, in fact, is what has led some recent writers to affirm that "a spirituality of the word emerges in some quarters as the best way to characterize the spirituality of priests. . . . [The priest's] responsibility to and for the word requires that the priest allow that word, according to Karl Rahner, 'to absorb and subject to itself the life of the priestly individual.'"[6]

Certainly in order to be fruitful, the *lectio* that informs spirituality and preaching must maintain a firm grasp of the first dimension mentioned in *Dei verbum* §12, namely the integral and concrete reality of the text in its historically conditioned particularity. Indeed, such a consideration is not even a characteristically modern one. The ancient rabbis focused perhaps even more than modern commentators on the minutest details of grammar, spelling, and vocalization of the sacred text, and in the same spirit, Origen exhorted his listeners to "observe each detail which has been written. For, if one knows how to dig into the depth, he will find a treasure in the details, and perhaps also, the precious jewels of the mysteries which lie hidden where they are not esteemed."[7] Some knowledge of historical background is often crucial in ascertaining the

5. Pope Benedict XVI, Address during the 14th General Congregation of the Synod of Bishops.

6. Raymond Studzinski, "Assimilating the Word: Priestly Spirituality and *Lectio Divina*," 70–91 in *Louvain Studies* 30, no. 1/2 (2005): 70. From Karl Rahner, Studzinski is citing "Priest and Poet," in *Theological Investigations*, vol. 3, trans. Karl H. Kruger and Boniface Kruger (New York: Crossroad, 1982), 313.

7. Origen, *Homilies on Genesis*, trans. Ronald E. Heine, *Homilies on Genesis and Exodus* (Washington, DC: Catholic University of America Press, 1982), homily 8, section 1, p. 136.

original impact of a story precisely for the sake of uncovering its timeless message: for example, as Frances M. Young has pointed out, some knowledge of the cultural tension between Jews and Samaritans in the first century is necessary in order to assist the twenty-first-century reader in understanding that the parable of the Good Samaritan is about more than merely kindness to strangers.[8] Seamus O'Connell adds insightfully: "Without a historical optic, contemporary readers of the Bible risk never tasting the 'otherness' of the Bible—in both Testaments—and being condemned to the interpretative shallows."[9] If such historical details pertain to the "body" of the text rather than to its soul or spirit, they are nevertheless as integral to its message as the Lord's physical body is to his work of the Redemption. Nor is it a question only of a quantitative balance between textual, historico-critical, and spiritual considerations of the text, since these may be so intricately intertwined as to be inseparable. Accordingly, it would be extremely difficult, and perhaps impossible, to outline *a priori* the kind of balance or integration between historico-critical and spiritual dimensions of exegesis that would best assist the reader to prepare for a *lectio* that will nourish personal prayer and preaching.

What this study sets out to do, then, is a rather simple experiment: namely, to examine the treatment of one chapter of the Gospel of John in three different commentaries exhibiting distinct methodologies, with a view to observing the ways in which each might be said to facilitate or hinder the practice of *lectio divina*. The biblical text treated in these commentaries and chosen for this experiment is the sixth chapter of John: an entire chapter rather than a single *pericopē*, because the exegetical method itself may affect one's way of organizing the text into distinct *pericopai*. The commentaries to be examined here are chosen on the basis of the different ways in which they focus on the historical dimension of the text—whether the history *of* the text or the history *in* the text. The goal here is to compare different respective methodologies with a view specifically to the contribution they might make to a *lectio* capable of informing spirituality and preaching. Each is chosen for the clarity, explicit articulation, and consistency of its respective methodological approach, which can then be seen as exemplified in its treatment of a specific chapter of John's Gospel. In the process, it can be seen that these three commentaries, in the order in which

8. Frances M. Young, "Ways of Reading the Bible: Can We Relativise the Historico-Critical Method and Rediscover a Biblical Spirituality?," *Doctrine and Life* 59, no. 9/10 (2009): 7–29, at 24.

9. Seamus O'Connell, "*Lectio Divina*: The Challenge in the Academic Setting," in *Doctrine and Life* 59, no. 9/10 (2009): 32–46, at 44.

they are considered (which is also the chronological order of their appearance) range from a relative absence (in Bultmann, in the commentary cited below) to a rather comprehensive inclusion (in Martin and Wright, likewise cited below) of the two methodological levels of biblical interpretation mentioned by Pope Benedict XVI. Furthermore, whatever the other respective benefits of each commentary may be, the ability of each one to nourish *lectio divina*, and also to serve as nourishment for prayer and as an aid to preaching, is enhanced to a corresponding degree in function of this integration.

Rudolf Bultmann's commentary on the Gospel of John was published by the author in German with no introduction,[10] but an introduction written by Walter Schmithals for the English translation tellingly poses a question that lies in the background of its whole methodology and profoundly affects its exegesis of specific texts, including chapter 6, which we are considering here; he states in fact that "there are reasons for doubting whether the Gospel itself has found entrance into the ecclesiastical tradition in the form intended by the author."[11] Indeed, we can see that Bultmann sometimes finds it useful to rearrange not only the order of the chapters but also the order of verses within a single chapter, and makes other choices which—regardless of their relative scholarly merit—seem to affect not only the reader's understanding of the text, but his relationship with it altogether, and sometimes in rather profound ways.

The next commentary chosen for consideration is Rudolf Schnackenburg's *The Gospel According to John*. Schnackenburg wishes his commentary to benefit from the soundest results of the historico-critical work done by scholars before him, including many Protestants, and in fact, some of the same types of analysis characteristic of Bultmann's exegesis are found again in his treatment of John 6. At the same time, Schnackenburg wants to be guided by the Catholic tradition, as he states: "I should like the commentary to make its contribution to the present state of studies, without abandoning Catholic tradition or the scientific method used by New Testament scholars of all confessions."[12]

Finally, we shall examine the commentary on the same chapter 6 of John's Gospel in the volume belonging to the Catholic Commentary on Sacred

10. Rudolf Bultmann, *Das Evangelium des Johannes* (Göttingen: Vandenhoeck & Ruprecht, 1941).

11. Walter Schmithals, introduction to *The Gospel of John: A Commentary*, by Rudolf Bultmann, trans. G. R. Beasley-Murray (Oxford: Basil Blackwell, 1971), 10.

12. Rudolf Schnackenburg, *The Gospel According to John*, vol. 1, trans. C. Hastings, F. McDonagh, D. Smith, and R. Foley (New York: Crossroad, 1987), 3. Originally published in German as *Das Johannesevangelium: [Volume] 2 Kommentar zu Kap. 5–12* (Freiburg: Herder, 2001).

Scripture by Francis Martin and William F. Wright IV, published by Baker Academic Press.[13] The main reason for this choice is that the commentary is recent enough to have incorporated explicitly among its methodological principles the unity of the exegetical and theological dimensions described by Pope Benedict in his address to the Synod and subsequently incorporated into the Post-Synodal Apostolic Exhortation *Verbum Domini*, as stated by Peter Williamson and Mary Healy in the Editors' Preface:

> Central to our approach are the principles taught by Vatican II: first, the use of historical and literary methods to discern what the biblical authors intended to express; second, prayerful theological reflection to understand the sacred text "in accord with the same Spirit by whom it was written"—that is, in the light of the content and unity of the whole of Scripture, the living tradition of the Church, and the analogy of faith.[14]

Rudolf Bultmann

In his commentary on the Fourth Gospel, Rudolf Bultmann begins his consideration of the larger section encompassing chapter 6 by expressing the conviction that the present order of chapters 5 and 6 cannot be the original one. Since chapter 5 takes place in Jerusalem, the setting of the events of chapter 6 "across the sea of Tiberias" (*peran tēs thalassēs tēs Tiberiados*) does not appear geographically coherent to Bultmann, as for others whom he follows, so he finds chapter 6 better suited to follow chapter 4, which does unfold in Galilee, while chapter 5 is seen by him as better suited to lead into chapters 7 and following, which unfold similarly in Jerusalem.[15]

Seemingly in some tension with this effort to rearrange the text for geographical and chronological plausibility is Bultmann's observation that instead of the multiplicity of small pieces of tradition characterizing the Synoptic accounts, the Gospel of John "gives his portrayal in a series of large detailed pictures. And even if he fits these pictures into a chronological scheme, the individual sections are still not intended as particular historical scenes, but as representative pictures of the revelation-event."[16] On the one hand, the present text supposedly cannot be the original one because it is historically and

13. Francis Martin and William F. Wright IV, *The Gospel of John*, CCSSc, ed. Peter S. Williamson and Mary Healy (Grand Rapids: Baker Academic, 2015).

14. Peter Williamson and Mary Healy, Editors' Preface to *The Gospel of John*, by Francis and Wright, 10.

15. Bultmann, *The Gospel of John*, 209.

16. Bultmann, *The Gospel of John*, 210.

chronologically implausible; on the other, the text is not considered to aim at such plausibility at all, but rather at the construction of a narrative intended simply to give a presumably fictitious form to a theological message. These two characterizations of the text seem mutually contradictory, but they have in common the presupposition that the text in its current form does not reliably provide the reader with dependable access to an actual historical event in which the divine Word reveals himself.

Similarly cited for rearrangement is the body of the text stretching from vv. 27–51a. According to Bultmann, the request for a sign in v. 30 ("What sign can you do, that we may see and believe in you?") is problematic in its present location since the miracle of the multiplication has just taken place. Bultmann states: "Clearly the Evangelist ignores the external situation and uses the feeding miracle, which he takes from the source, as a symbolic picture for the main idea of the revelation discourse, namely that Jesus gives the bread of life."[17] He also holds that v. 36 ("Although you have seen me, [you] do not believe") must be misplaced because the chiding for unbelief is unwarranted here "before the question of the believers' assurance of salvation has been discussed in vv. 37–40."[18] For these and for other reasons he concludes that the original order might be 27, 34, 35, 30–33, 47–51a, 41–46, 36–40, while leaving out vv. 28–29 as "a detached fragment added by the editor after v. 27 by association with the word *ergazesthai*," and then he proceeds to comment on the passage in this order, admitting that v. 28 must be Johannine, since it has the style of the Evangelist; yet he concludes that it must come from some other dialogue, of which nothing else has apparently been preserved.[19]

For Bultmann, v. 29 ("Jesus answered and said to them, 'This is the work of God, that you believe in the one he sent.'") provides the crucial Johannine affirmation of Jesus; the assertion that the human response called forth by God's word consists not in "a series of isolated achievements, but properly speaking in the persistent attitude of his new being. . . . [A] man finds his true being not in what he himself achieves, but in submission to what God works . . . , that is to say, in what, by faith, he allows to happen to himself."[20] Bultmann is deeply convinced, then, of the power of the divine word to call upon the reader or hearer and to elicit his or her faith, characterized by him not as any notional assent but as an existential attitude. But for him, the call of the transcendent God is found

17. Bultmann, *The Gospel of John*, 218.
18. Bultmann, *The Gospel of John*, 221.
19. Bultmann, *The Gospel of John*, 221–222.
20. Bultmann, *The Gospel of John*, 222.

hidden beneath and behind the text rather than within it, and the response that he finds it to elicit from the reader is characterized by profound commitments and attitudes rather than by discrete actions or acts of assent to any specific affirmation of historical or dogmatic truth.

When he comes to vv. 51b–58, Bultmann seems as thoroughly convinced as any Catholic apologist that these verses as presently formulated are intended to describe the believer's contact with the Body and Blood of Christ through the Eucharistic elements, but he holds this section to be the work of a later redactor whose perspective is not only different from that of the remainder of chapter 6 but even in conflict with it. He takes due note of the substitution of *trōgein* (i.e., the more graphic "gnaw") for *phagein* as further proof of the intention: "It is a matter of real eating and not simply of some sort of spiritual participation."[21] For example, Bultmann considers the characterization of the Eucharistic reception of the Body and Blood of Christ as the cause of the believer's resurrection (v. 54: "Whoever eats my flesh and drinks my blood has eternal life, and I will raise him on the last day") to be more reminiscent of the thought of Saint Ignatius of Antioch, who in the early second century characterized the Eucharist as the *pharmakon athanasias* (the drug of immortality), than of that found earlier in chapter 6 of John.[22] According to Bultmann, the authentically Johannine position is that it is Jesus himself, rather than "this bread," who is the bread of life: "In all this there is no need for a sacramental act, by means of which the believer must make the life his own."[23] When Bultmann asserts that "This explains why many of the earlier exegetes denied that vv. 51b–58 referred to the Eucharist," the "earlier exegetes" to whom he is referring are not the Fathers but earlier twentieth-century exegetes.[24] Furthermore, he even suggests that the editor's insertion of 51b–58 has *weakened* the original impact of the Evangelist's account: the *sklēros logos* and the *skandalon* without the insertion would have been the very reality of the Incarnation itself, which "always remains a *skandalon*." But "Here it has been reduced to the idea that the hearers cannot understand that Jesus is speaking of the Lord's Supper."[25]

21. Bultmann, *The Gospel of John*, 236. On p. 234 Bultmann adds the observation that since the drinking of Jesus' blood is mentioned here (for the first time) along with the bread, the reference can *only* be to the Church's celebration of the Eucharist.

22. Bultmann, *The Gospel of John*, 218–219.

23. Bultmann, *The Gospel of John*, 219, including n2, and 234–235, with n9. Bultmann sees the Johannine view, by supposed contrast, as evidenced in passages such as 3:18 *passim*; 5:24 *passim*; 11:25 *passim*, in all of which it is faith alone that ensures salvation and resurrection.

24. Bultmann, *The Gospel of John*, 219n3.

25. Bultmann, *The Gospel of John*, 237.

The text, as Bultmann sees it, does intend to elicit from the hearer a profound act of faith and commitment, but his assessment of the dialogue between the text and its hearer has jettisoned any historical moorings not only on the side of the text, but on the side of the hearer as well. In other words, the text that supposedly calls out to the hearer is not the text before him on the page, but one that has been reconstructed through painstaking analysis described above. And the life of the hearer thus addressed is not the external one supported by the rites that supposedly developed later in the Eucharistic celebration and were lived out in concrete deeds, but rather a disembodied interior life unsullied by the sacramental ritual (since, as we shall see, vv. 51b–58 are supposedly the work of a later redactor) or by trust in external deeds.

In Bultmann's estimation, it is not only in chapter 6 that this supposed redactor's re-casting of an existential commitment into sacramental terminology is to be found. As he outlines it, "Just as in ch. 3 the editor felt the lack of any reference to baptism, and added it himself, so too he did in ch. 6 with reference to the Eucharist."[26] Bultmann even supposes an outright *anti-sacramental bias* on the part of the original Evangelist, referring the reader to his own commentary in chapter 13 where he supposes that 13:10 ("Whoever has bathed has no need except to have his feet washed, for he is clean all over; so you are clean, but not all") is "not only directed against all attempts to secure a guarantee of salvation by means other than faith, but more particularly against the introduction of special means of purification, namely washings or baptisms."[27] Either it is directed against all post-baptismal washings, "Or on the contrary, the service Jesus performs, through the word and as the word, is considered to be fundamentally opposed to every form of sacramental purification, baptism included."[28] Bultmann suggests a total lack of sacramentalism in the Gospel as originally conceived by the Evangelist; at least, in his estimation, "If the Evangelist did come to terms with the sacraments, he can only have understood them in the sense that in them the word is made present in a special way . . . In conclusion, it would be difficult to maintain that the foot-washing represents baptism; it portrays, rather, Jesus' service, which he performs through the word, as the word, on behalf of his own."[29]

How might use be made of such a commentary as this in one's preparation for biblical prayer, and in particular, for *lectio divina?* It would certainly

26. Bultmann, *The Gospel of John*, 220.
27. Bultmann, *The Gospel of John*, 471.
28. Bultmann, *The Gospel of John*, 471–472.
29. Bultmann, *The Gospel of John*, 471–473.

be unfair to Bultmann to suggest that he sees the Bible—and specifically, this chapter of the Gospel of John—as posing no spiritual challenge to the reader or that it contains nothing of spiritual nourishment. Certain key affirmations and challenges in the text—such as Jesus' chiding of his hearers' unbelief in v. 36 and his identification of their belief as precisely the "work" that God wants from them—are placed within a new sequence by Bultmann precisely in order to "restore" to them (in Bultmann's estimate) their original impact. It seems that he wishes to distance the earlier part of the chapter with its spiritualized notion of "eating" the Bread of Life, reminiscent of Old Testament Wisdom's banquet, from the contents of the subsequent verses because he believes that in these latter verses a redactor's hand has weakened this message by interposing elements of ecclesial ritual, providing what Bultmann seems to regard as a more facile means of accessing the "bread" being offered, thus diluting the impact of the original message.

For *lectio divina*, however, Bultmann's overall manner of treating the text seems rather unsuited as preparation, since the concrete reality of the text in its encounter with the reader fares no better in Bultmann's estimation than the sacramental rituals whose presence by allusion he finds so intrusive in vv. 51b–58. For a Catholic in particular, Bultmann's treatment can be disturbing because it severs the essential link—indeed, the identity—between Jesus himself and the Eucharist, suggesting that in order to have unencumbered access to the former, one must dispense with the latter. Through Bultmann's interpretation, the reader is presumably directed toward an existential encounter with Christ, but with a Christ who is disembodied and ahistorical. Bultmann's reconstructed text can be pondered, perhaps, and the ideas that he finds mostly *behind* that text can be considered and grappled with, but the text itself cannot be read and savored in prayer, because it has not been left intact. It seems fair to say that for Bultmann, the text itself, as it presently stands, could not be regarded as a living "body" of the incarnate Word, to use Origen's terminology.[30]

Rudolf Schnackenburg

At the beginning of his commentary on the Gospel of John, Rudolf Schnackenburg frankly admits the challenges presented by much of twentieth-century

30. Cf. Hans Urs von Balthasar, *Origen: Spirit and Fire*, trans. Robert J. Daly (Washington, DC: Catholic University of America Press, 1984), 86–94. Origen, "First Principles: Book IV," in *Origen: An Exhortation to Martyrdom, Prayer and Selected Works*, CWS (New York: Paulist, 1979), 182–183.

exegesis to the reader's task of finding the historically real Jesus Christ in this Gospel's pages. He affirms: "The tension which is now so strongly felt between 'faith and history', 'history and myth', 'historical knowledge and the understanding of faith', comes out perhaps more strongly than elsewhere in the Gospel of John. Every commentary on it represents a scientific decision and a personal confession of faith."[31] But Schnackenburg nevertheless wishes to draw upon the benefits of modern historico-critical research while remaining firmly within the framework of the Catholic tradition.

As Bultmann and others before him had done, Schnackenburg argues that chapters 5 and 6 should be transposed to regain their original and more comprehensible sequence and impact; for him, the proper sequence of chapters and parts of chapters should be: chapter 6; chapters 5 and 7:15–24; chapter 7 except for vv. 15–24; chapter 8; and then chapters 9–12 in their canonical order, and thus his commentary proceeds through the text in this sequence.[32] He cites the work of other exegetes, mentioning Tatian as an early proponent of the transposition of chapters 5 and 6 even while discounting the scientific importance of this decision, noting that the second-century author did so as part of an effort to harmonize the Gospels and not for exegetical reasons. Among more recent scholars, he notes that the reordering was proposed already by N. Mann in 1773 and had been followed by many others, being rejected, however, by C. H. Dodd and C. K. Barrett.[33] In fact, like Tatian, Schnackenburg finds that a greater harmony with the Synoptic accounts does come about through the transposition of the chapters, and he adds this argument to the geographical and chronological reasons for the transposition already seen above in the commentary of Bultmann.[34] Following upon chapter 4 and coming before the passage to Jerusalem in the newly ordered text, chapter 6 receives from Bultmann the heading of "The Climax of the Galilean Ministry."[35]

Schnackenburg's willingness to intervene upon the canonical shape of the text, however, is somewhat more restrained than Bultmann's. When considering vv. 27–51a, he opines without much discussion that "Attempts at critical surgery on the grand composition of Chapter 6 are undesirable."[36] He also

31. Schnackenburg, *The Gospel According to John*, 1:3.

32. Schnackenburg, *The Gospel According to John*, 2:4–9.

33. Schnackenburg, *The Gospel According to John*, 2:5.

34. Schnackenburg, *The Gospel According to John*, 2:5–7.

35. Schnackenburg, *The Gospel According to John*, 2:10.

36. Schnackenburg, *The Gospel According to John*, 2:12. Schnackenburg does remark that in making such a decision he is disagreeing with notable authors such as Wellhausen, Spitta, and Hirsch: cf. also p. 440n7.

pays great attention to the unity of the canon and thus to the Old Testament allusions that abound in the Gospel of John, including chapter 6. Similarly to other commentators who had suggested that vv. 51b–58 exhibit a very different notion of the Bread of Life from that found in the rest of the chapter, Schnackenburg writes of the connection between v. 35 (i.e., Jesus' first identification of himself as the "bread of life" and his promise of unending satiety to all who come to him) and Wisdom texts such as Proverbs 9:5, Sirach 24:21, and 51:24.[37] But he pays more attention than those other commentators he cites to inter-testamental parallels and allusions in general: for example, the typology linking the ascent of Jesus on the mountain in chapter 6 with Moses' ascent of Sinai, the multiplication of loaves with the manna, references to Jesus as "the Prophet" with Moses' foretelling in Deuteronomy 18:15 of a prophet to come, the grumbling of the Jews to the Israelites' grumbling against Moses, the barley loaves with the story of Elisha in 2 Kings 4:42–44, and Jesus' walking on the water in 6:19 as reminiscent of God's power shown in the Old Testament over the forces of chaos and death, finding resonance also in Psalm 77:20 ("your way went through the sea, your path through the mighty waters; your footsteps were unseen").[38] In the believer's being "drawn" by the Father to Jesus in v. 44, Schnackenburg finds echoes of Jeremiah 31:3 ("With everlasting love I have loved you, and therefore I have drawn you into my mercy") and Hosea 11:4 ("I drew them with bands of man . . . with strings of love").[39] And in the verb *makhesthai* ("to quarrel") in v. 52, he finds hints of the frequent Old Testament theme of the divine-human *rîb* found in passages such as Exodus 17:2 and Numbers 20:3.[40]

Compared to Bultmann in whose work the dichotomy between the spiritual word and the concrete sign seemed to have hardened into a rather sharp dualism, Schnackenburg sees no mutually exclusive choice to be made between material bread and the spiritual "bread of life"; instead, he focuses on the depth of meaning lying beneath the surface of things, but signified and contained therein. Commenting on Jesus' criticism of the crowd in v. 26, he observes: "The experience of feeding did not lead these people to a deeper vision. Their eating of 'the loaves' (note difference from 23) gave them pleasure, but it was enough for them to have their stomachs filled. Their thoughts and their

37. Schnackenburg, *The Gospel According to John*, 2:44–45.
38. Schnackenburg, *The Gospel According to John*, 2:10, 14, 16, 18–19, 26, 29, and 49.
39. Schnackenburg, *The Gospel According to John*, 2:50.
40. Schnackenburg, *The Gospel According to John*, 2:60.

searching have no higher object."[41] Schackenburg's language here seems more suggestive of a sacramental economy than of dualism, and presages correctly the fact that he will provide a far more appreciative treatment than Bultmann of the contents of vv. 51b (or c, depending on the author) to 58.

Schnackenburg gives his assent to the characterization of vv. 51b–58 as an "editorial expansion," pointing out that the main argument for this position has always been that the "completely symbolic attitude of the bread discourse in 6:31–51 . . . contrasts with the 'sacramental realism' of the eucharistic verses."[42] In rather noncommittal fashion, he cites the opinion of some commentators that the treatment in these verses of the Eucharist as the medium of heavenly powers and gifts *conflicts* "with the view of the Evangelist, who allows only faith in the revealer sent by God to be necessary for salvation."[43] Similarly, he cites Georg Richter's observation that the "immanence formula" in v. 56 ("Whoever eats my flesh and drinks my blood remains in me, and I in him") is reserved by the Evangelist for the relationship between Jesus and the Father, while the expression "to have life in oneself" in v. 54 is reserved by the Evangelist for God and Christ (i.e., in 1:4 and 5:26), thereby implying that these verses using such language of the Eucharist are unlikely to be part of the same fabric of which the earlier verses are woven.[44] For his own part, Schnackenburg is at least careful to assert that he sees no intention to allude to the Eucharist in the earlier parts of Jesus' discourse in chapter 6. In the exhortation in v. 27, to work not for perishable food but for the food that endures to eternal life, Schnackenburg sees no Eucharistic allusion but interprets the verse in light of its proximity to 4:14 (newly achieved by the rearrangement of the order of chapters), which had referred to the water that wells up to eternal life. Since he sees no Eucharistic allusion in 4:14, he considers it unfeasible here as well.[45]

Apart from vv. 51b–58, Schnackenburg does not make many excisions from

41. Schnackenburg, *The Gospel According to John*, 2:35. This theme is closely related to the many instances of irony in the Gospel of John that Schnackenburg mentions: for example in his treatment of v. 42, where he points out the irony of the Jews' thinking they know about Jesus' origins even though they see only the surface reality and not the deeper truth. The contrast between the "loaves" and what is found in v. 23 refers to the singular *ton arton* as compared to plural *tōn artōn*.

42. Schnackenburg, *The Gospel According to John*, 2:56.

43. Schnackenburg, *The Gospel According to John*, 2:57.

44. Schnackenburg, *The Gospel According to John*, 2:57.

45. Schnackenburg, *The Gospel According to John*, 2:36. As far as it goes, the interplay of v. 27 with the promise in 4:14 is of course plausible, especially because both are followed by plea for the enduring food or drink apparently based on a materialistic misunderstanding of Jesus' words: cf. Schnackenburg's treatment on p. 43.

the canonical text of chapter 6 on the basis of a surmised "non-Johannine" provenance, though he does follow a number of other commentators in doing so for v. 23, stating that it "can be recognized with some certainty as non-Johannine."[46] He cites in particular, in support of this decision, the reasons given by J. H. Bernard, one that a redactor had seen as necessary because of the prior mention of only one boat, but also because of the words *eukharistēsantos* and the singular *artos* indicating an intention to insert sacramental significance here, a tendency "which Jn. studiously avoids in his narrative," according to Bernard.[47] In other words, Schnackenburg sounds in unison with the many other exegetes who take care to assert that vv. 35–51a cannot have been crafted originally with any intention to allude to the Eucharist.

Even so, Schnackenburg is not so convinced that the "editorial expansion" must be regarded as a very late addition, and goes so far as to open the door to the suggestion that perhaps it could even be the work of the same Evangelist, who might have wished to have the treatment of the Bread of Life to end with the sacramental reference, or to correct misunderstandings of it.[48] In handling this question, Schnackenburg does not consider linguistic or stylistic arguments to be conclusive, even though he strongly affirms that the language in this section goes beyond the metaphor of the earlier verses.[49] He characterizes v. 57 ("As the living Father has sent me and I live through the Father, so he who eats me will live through me") as thoroughly Johannine in vocabulary and style, and argues also that the mention of the "last day" in v. 62 seems more characteristic of a Semitic background than other later, Greek texts that spoke of the Eucharist as conveying *athanasia*.[50] Still, he does seem to give significant weight to the suggestion that the eucharistic references are intended to counteract certain Docetist tendencies currently being felt within the community being addressed, a theory that would seem suggestive of a later time than that of the Evangelist.[51]

46. Schnackenburg, *The Gospel According to John*, 2:33.

47. J. H. Bernard, *St. John*, vol. 1, ed. S. R. Driver, A. Plummer, and C. A. Briggs, ICC (Edinburgh: T & T Clark, 1997), 189. Bernard further points out that *ho kyrios* here is atypical of the Johannine narrative. Like Schnackenburg, Bernard is sparing in his willingness to make such excisions. The only other part of the Gospel that he characterizes with such confidence as non-Johannine is the pericope of the adulteress in 7:53–8:11, while he suggests that perhaps 11:2 and 12:16 might also be non-Johannine insertions (p. xxxiii). Similarly to Schnackenburg, he transposes chapters 5 and 6 (p. 171 *passim*, having provided his reasons in pp. xvi–xix).

48. Schnackenburg, *The Gospel According to John*, 2:58–59.

49. Schnackenburg, *The Gospel According to John*, 2:56.

50. Schnackenburg, *The Gospel According to John*, 2:62.

51. Schnackenburg, *The Gospel According to John*, 2:61.

In the final analysis, Schnackenburg is able to attribute to chapter 6 a far greater degree of unity than Bultmann does. In the verses of the "editorial expansion" found in vv. 51bc–58, he notes that "while the primary allusion is back to the Eucharist, there is also a reference back to the metaphor; the eating of the eucharistic bread is the final acting out of the eating mentioned in the text of v. 31."[52]

For one who would turn to Schnackenburg as part of the preparation for *lectio divina*, then, there seems to be much more of the text left intact in its canonical shape than remained after Bultmann's analysis, which could be described more appropriately as wholesale reconstruction than as surgery. Behind Schnackenburg's frequent observation of the affinity between a given Johannine passage and its Old Testament antecedents, there does seem to be implicit acknowledgment of a single divine voice speaking through both Testaments. Even though his methodology remains largely diachronic, the canon as such remains always in the background as a hermeneutical key for Schnackenburg, much more than it had been for Bultmann. For this reason he is generally more hesitant than Bultmann to conclude that the present text needs to be rearranged in order to speak with its "original" power to today's reader.

Even so, one might legitimately wonder whether Schnackenburg's deference to the unity of the canonical text nevertheless stands at odds with some of the presuppositions of the scholarship on which he relies in analyzing the same text. Seemingly missing from the analysis of some of the authors whom Schnackenburg cites (not the least of whom is Bultmann himself) is any evident conviction that the unified message emerging from the integral canonical text is one that is foreseen by the *primary* author of the same text, God himself. From the perspective of *this* Author, it is unthinkable that the "bread of life" in vv. 35–51a could be unrelated to the Eucharist, or that the emphasis on reception of the Body *and* Blood of the Lord in the latter part of v. 51 and the succeeding verses could be an afterthought in relation to the rest of the chapter. Schnackenburg's fidelity to Catholic Tradition affects his filtering of conclusions more than it does his methodology, even if it does temper the latter somewhat.

Francis Martin and William Wright IV

In the commentary on the Gospel of John appearing in 2015 as part of the Catholic Commentary on Sacred Scripture, the treatment of chapter 6 begins by situating this chapter within the subsection of the Gospel extending from 5:1

52. Schnackenburg, *The Gospel According to John*, 2:65.

to 10:42, said to treat of Jesus' relation to some of the major Jewish liturgical feasts. They are the Sabbath (5:1–47), Passover (6:1–71), Tabernacles (7:1–10:21), and Dedication (10:22–42). Thus, the commentary seeks to understand the text within the framework of its present canonical structure rather than to re-order it on the basis of a conjectured original structure presumably changed subsequently by an editor or even by happenstance.[53] The basic structure of chapter 6 as presented in the canonical text is outlined thus:

> There is deep reflection on Jewish liturgical traditions and on many biblical themes: the tree of life in Eden, the manna in the wilderness, Wisdom's invitation to share in her food. These Old Testament realities help us to understand Jesus and the gift of his body and blood on the cross and in the Eucharist. Through many allusions, we are led to appreciate Jesus' gift of himself to the Father and to us. Jesus' self-gift was actualized in his passion and is made present as our nourishment in the Eucharist, our foretaste of the heavenly banquet.[54]

This commentary does not ignore apparent textual discrepancies necessitating a caution to the reader against an over-simplistic reading of the text; it points out, for example, that the apparent citation regarding Moses in 6:31, "He gave them bread from heaven to eat," is not an actual quote as such, but points out that its assertion is closest to Exodus 16:4 in which the gift of manna is announced as "bread from heaven."[55] This commentary, however, refrains from drawing upon any internal textual discrepancies to suggest that the text must be fragmented into pieces to recover its original sense. It acknowledges, for example, a certain puzzlement occasioned by the single boat in v. 22 and the arrival of the other boats in v. 23, but does not dwell on these to make conjectures about the redaction of the text; instead, it simply takes the narration at face value. It likewise notes the use of the word for giving thanks as a form of the verb *eucharisteō* and alerts the reader to that fact in a footnote, but for a purpose quite different from the other commentaries treated above. What the commentary seems to consider useful to the reader is the Eucharistic connection being made in the text's present canonical form, rather than the implications that might be drawn from this connection about the development of the present text.[56] The absence (or at least the sparing amount) of redaction criti-

53. Francis and Wright, *The Gospel of John*, 113. The outline of the list of Jewish feasts is found on p. 96.

54. Francis and Wright, *The Gospel of John*, 113.

55. Francis and Wright, *The Gospel of John*, 122.

56. Francis and Wright, *The Gospel of John*, 120.

cism in which the commentary engages does not seem in any way to indicate a dismissive attitude toward such analysis as a scholarly pursuit; rather, this commentary is evidently intended for a readership whose purpose would not be served by over-emphasizing redactional concerns, a readership that wishes instead to utilize any helpful insights of exegetical science, but to assume toward the biblical text the posture of a recipient of its contents rather than an evaluator of its present form through diachronic analysis.

The many allusions and other points of contact between this chapter and the Old Testament are noted in this commentary as in Schnackenburg's. The connection between Jesus' ascent of the mountain in 6:3 and Moses' ascent of the mountain is highlighted, as is the resonance between the mention of the barley loaves here and in the story of Elisha in 2 Kings.[57] The abundance of grass mentioned in v. 10 is seen as evocative of Psalm 23:2: "In green pastures he makes me lie down."[58] The mention of Passover in 6:4 is fleshed out in its significance for the New Covenant: "This notice indicates John's concern to unfold the spiritual relationship between Jesus and the exodus, the origin of Passover, in God's plan, especially God's loving-kindness for his people as shown in his providing them with food in the wilderness."[59] The promise of never hungering or thirsting is seen as evocative of similar promises of the fullness that comes from listening to God in Isaiah 49:10; 48:21, and 55:2–3.[60] And the murmuring of the Jews in 6:41, 43 is also connected here with that of the Israelites in Moses' time.[61] To the many allusions to Old Testament imagery seen in Schnackenburg, this one adds a reference that he does not seem to have noted: in the promise that "whoever eats this bread will live forever," there is seen an allusion to the tree of life in the garden of Eden. Whereas other commentators had preoccupied themselves with the presumed editorial insertion of this pericope because they saw it as a reflection of the early patristic references to the Eucharist as a *pharmakon athanasias*, the present commentator, unencumbered by such preoccupations, is able to find its resonance elsewhere within the biblical canon.[62]

Perhaps the most striking difference in the structure of the treatment of chapter 6 found in this commentary compared to those above is the fact that here, vv. 48–59 are taken as a unit. Instead of dividing the text on the basis of

57. Francis and Wright, *The Gospel of John*, 114–115.
58. Francis and Wright, *The Gospel of John*, 115.
59. Francis and Wright, *The Gospel of John*, 114.
60. Francis and Wright, *The Gospel of John*, 124.
61. Francis and Wright, *The Gospel of John*, 126.
62. Francis and Wright, *The Gospel of John*, 128.

theories about its diachronic composition, the commentary looks only at the flow of the present canonical text, and notes very reasonably that vv. 48–51a has already drawn a contrast between the bread from heaven received in the past and the bread being presently given, which the present form of the text clearly identifies as the Eucharistic Body and Blood of the Lord.[63] Taking this not as the intrusion of an afterthought but as an essential feature of the canonical text, the commentator considers the explicitly eucharistic reference here not as a deflation of a more expansive and spiritual theme found elsewhere in the chapter, but as the ultimate sign of the enduring accessibility of this very heavenly bread.[64]

In this commentary, after each pericope and before the commentary given on it, cross-references are given providing links to illustrative texts in the Old and New Testaments, a section of the Catechism of the Catholic Church covering areas of doctrine touched upon by the themes raised in the biblical section, and if the section appears in the Lectionary for Mass, a mention of where it occurs, such as a given Sunday of the year, a votive Mass, etc.[65] Footnotes direct the reader to contemporary literature where fuller studies of important themes are more thoroughly covered; one example is Wayne Meeks's 1967 study of the Jewish tradition noting the convergence in Moses of the roles of Prophet and King, *The Prophet-King: Moses Traditions and the Johannine Christology*.[66] Monuments of ecclesial tradition that resonate with given elements in the biblical text are sometimes included in boxes within the text; for example, near the beginning of the Bread of Life Discourse a box is provided mentioning Saint Ignatius of Antioch's hunger for the bread of heaven in his Letter to the Romans. The patristic reference is perhaps rather tangentially related to the actual words of the text here, but is potentially fruitful in providing an ecclesial instance of the same hunger for the true bread of heaven mentioned in the text.[67] Furthermore, the commentary does not hesitate to draw applications to contemporary issues exemplifying directions that might be taken in a homiletic exposition of the passage: for example, Jesus' avoidance in 6:15 of allowing himself to be made a king—at least according to preexisting categories—is compared to the Church's challenge of not allowing herself to be "modernized" by teaching a system of moral categories set by the world rather than by God.[68]

63. Francis and Wright, *The Gospel of John*, 127.
64. Francis and Wright, *The Gospel of John*, 130.
65. Francis and Wright, *The Gospel of John*, 114 *passim*.
66. Francis and Wright, *The Gospel of John*, 116.
67. Francis and Wright, *The Gospel of John*, 123.
68. Francis and Wright, *The Gospel of John*, 117.

Suggestions for further theological development of specific themes in the text are not lacking either. In the treatment of vv. 54 and 55, the reader is referred even in the text of the commentary to the text of the Catechism (§1391); then, in a box, there is given a quote from the hymn of Saint Thomas Aquinas, *Panis Angelicus*; and mention is made of Henri de Lubac's statement that "The Eucharist makes the Church," and the centrality of the Eucharist in the life of the Church is mentioned.[69] Similarly, in the treatment of vv. 64–65, a section from Saint Augustine's *Tractates on John* is provided regarding the theme of being drawn by the Father.[70]

Certainly this is a very different kind of commentary from what we have seen throughout the twentieth century. To some, perhaps this is not commentary at all because it goes beyond a mere *lectio* of the text to suggest avenues toward *meditatio* and *contemplatio*. Indeed, this difference between various commentaries perhaps gives evidence of a variation between them in the very meaning of exegesis: does exegesis pertain only to the *lectio*, or do *meditatio*, *oratio*, and *contemplatio* enter into or overlap with its task?

A section entitled "Reflection and Application," in fact, complements each section of commentary, and it is in this section that most of the reflections mentioned above are found. Such an arrangement helps to make clear that the giving of such suggestions do not constitute an intrusion into the commentary on the text that could be accused of eisegetical treatment; rather, it is a decision within an edited commentary not to stop with *lectio* or with the literal sense, but to provide some bridge leading toward the other three parts of *lectio divina* and the various spiritual senses of Scripture.

Conclusions

The comparison of the respective exegetical methodologies of the three commentaries considered above leads first of all to a conclusion that it would be impossible to rank them with respect to each other, because the task that each has set out to achieve is very different from that of each of the other two. Nor are they intended for the same type of audience; the first two are envisioned for a more scholarly readership of biblical specialists, while the third is expressly intended for an educated but non-specialized audience. However, each one has been clear about its goal and its method of reaching it, and in each case the stated goal might have been adjusted for a given level of knowledge

69. Francis and Wright, *The Gospel of John*, 129–131.
70. Francis and Wright, *The Gospel of John*, 133.

and specialization. Furthermore, *lectio divina* and homiletics are tasks that must likewise be adjusted to suit various readers and diverse congregations. Even so, it does seem that there are certain *methodological* considerations that have emerged—some by representation and others by deficit—as being relevant in the choice of exegetical works and commentaries to prepare one for these tasks.

The first consideration that has clearly emerged for consideration in the methodology of an appropriate commentary regards the posture the commentator assumes and engenders before the biblical text in its present canonical shape. Considerations of source and redaction criticism are not entirely without interest to an attentive reader and interpreter of the sacred word, but a commentary characterized by a methodology of radical reconstruction of the text shows a clear emphasis or even exclusive focus upon its *human* authorship, so that the reader is likely to become distracted in the attempt to hear specifically the divine message found not only behind the canonical text, but in it. For purposes of preparing *lectio divina* and homilies, this was an area of weakness of Bultmann's methodology and to some extent also of Schnackenburg's, but a strength of Martin and Wright, in particular.

Attention given in the commentary to the unity of the two Testaments, on the other hand, and to the mutual resonance between the text under consideration and elements found in the other Testament, is already in itself a clear indication that the exegetical work has in its focus a transcendent word underlying both and remaining unchanging even as it is progressively revealed. This aspect, relatively absent in Bultmann's analysis of John 6, was found much more strongly in Schnackenburg's and in Martin and Wright's.

Whatever the specific qualities that give it expression, another feature of a commentary that seems very helpful for our chosen purposes is a manifest conviction on the part of the author that the biblical word has something transformative to accomplish in its hearer. It is not intended merely to inform him or to satisfy his historical curiosity, but to challenge him and to change his life. For all his defects in other aspects relevant to our purposes, Bultmann must be given his due on this score; there does sometimes seem to be some discontinuity between the challenge that he finds in the text and the actual words that it presents, but the challenge and the transformative power are held by him to be present. Schnackenburg's analysis of the text, on the other hand—at least as it pertains to John 6—seems a bit lacking in this characteristic, while that of Martin and Wright, on the other hand, not only grapples with the challenges posed to the reader by the text but even goes so far as to propose themes that could be incorporated into actual homilies.

While a commentary's restraint in expressing any confessional commitments might be the good fruit of an inter-confessional project and serve as an ecumenical tool, the same restraint seems perhaps to limit its fruitfulness in preparing one for *lectio divina* and for homiletics. These seem more fully served by a commentary that not only amplifies the text's message using philological, historical, sociological, and other tools, but also takes note of the ecclesial "acoustics" surrounding its proclamation—namely those elements of tradition and culture that assist the reader to *hear* the word together with believers of all times and places in the Church. The art, poetry, hymnody, magisterial documents, liturgical prayers, popular devotions, and the lives of Saints who have been touched by the word all constitute features that can be relevant and helpful for the prayerful hearing and faithful expounding of God's word, and due attention to them in biblical hermeneutics is strongly suggested by the description given in *Dei verbum*, §12, in Pope Benedict's intervention at the Synod of Bishops, and in *Verbum Domini*. Of the three commentaries we have considered, only that of Francis and Wright has really set out to do this, because their methodology itself has been formed by those sources. It is to be hoped that further studies will begin to appear in the years to come that will similarly aim at such a unity of the historical and spiritual methodological levels of exegesis called for by *Dei verbum*, §12, outlined more explicitly in *Verbum Domini*, §35 and in the interventions of Pope Benedict XVI, and even exemplified by his own work in *Jesus of Nazareth*.[71]

As noted at the beginning of this paper, the three commentaries considered represent three distinct points along a continuum ranging from a relative absence to a rather comprehensive inclusion of Pope Benedict's "second methodological level" of reading the text in the context of the unity of the whole canon of inspired Scripture and in the light of ecclesial Tradition, as outlined by *Dei verbum*, §12. The specific observations just cited, then, exemplify the consequences of such a methodological choice in the usefulness of a commentary for *lectio divina* as well as for priestly formation and the pastoral use of the Bible. Along with other important factors comprising the relative quality of a given commentary, then, its relative degree of integration of this important methodological level will certainly constitute one important criterion of its usefulness for seminarians and priests.

71. Pope Benedict XVI, *Jesus of Nazareth*, trans. Philip J. Whitmore, 3 vols., (New York: Doubleday, 2007–2012).

Lectio Divina Fosters Growth and Formation

Konrad Schaefer, OSB

The present article on "the role of exegesis in the *lectio* of *lectio divina* with an eye to growth and formation"[1] is divided into part one, the theological underpinnings of *lectio divina*, and part two, a pedagogical consideration. As we will see, the leaven of the practice of *lectio* is kneaded into the lives of all prayerful Bible readers.

Part One: Theological Underpinnings of *Lectio Divina*

Might we say that music is language with two natures? An analysis of acoustics, resonances and intervals, string, wind, or percussion vibration, and the knowledge of music theory fail to provide a thorough appreciation of a musical score. Musicology does not capture the spiritual nature of the subject. What music communicates cannot be reduced to a formal analysis, without losing something of its essence. For music to be true to itself and its content, it needs to be performed, heard, and interpreted. Music, like the Word of God in human language, has two natures, the physical score, sound, the instrument and the art of the musician, which is coupled with the second nature, the spirit of the performing art.[2]

In the approach to the Word of God, the limitations of historical criticism are supplemented by reflection and prayer, in order for the study to build a bridge to the message. As a person approaches the Word of God, veneration

1. This topic was requested by Fr. Scott Carl, the organizer of the 2017 Quinn Biblical Conference. Cf. p. 2 of the present volume.

2. Frances Young, *Virtuoso Theology: The Bible and Interpretation* (Cleveland: Pilgrim Press, 1993), 22, presents the analogy.

or "fear"—in the biblical sense—is essential.[3] What about the relationship between reading or interpreting the Bible and the resonance of the Word of God in the interpreter's life? Early Church theologians and contemporary Church documents value this mysterious relation.

Double Mystery: The Divine and Human Word

The essence of sacred Scripture is human and divine, the timeless Word of God composed in human language,[4] and, if biblical study and criticism is to go beyond mere literary appreciation, the interpreter ultimately works from the stance of faith.[5] Without the appreciation of the divine quality of the Word, he or she risks that the hermeneutic fall short of the intent of the text, and one's conclusions may be reduced to a literal interpretation. On the other hand, without the appreciation of the human component, we risk our conversion and prayer not having sufficient foundation or our theological life not taking roots in the nature of our humus.

Saint Augustine complements the Second Vatican Council's teaching: "God speaks in sacred Scripture through men in human fashion."[6] *Dei verbum* continues:

> In sacred Scripture, therefore, while the truth and holiness of God always remain intact, the marvelous "condescension" of eternal wisdom is clearly shown, "that we may learn the gentle kindness of God, which words cannot express, and how far He has gone in adapting His language with thoughtful concern for our weak human nature." For the words of God, expressed in human language, have been made like human discourse, just as the Word of the eternal Father, when He took to Himself the weak flesh of humanity, became like other men.[7]

3. May we understand the "*fear* of the Lord that is the beginning of wisdom" as respectful love or loving respect, a consciousness of the distance that separates and in the same breath an attraction toward the object of fear?

4. Cf. *Dei verbum,* §11: "In composing the sacred books, God chose men and while employed by Him they made use of their powers and abilities, so that with Him acting in them and through them, they, as true authors, consigned to writing everything and only those things which He wanted." *The Documents of Vatican II,* trans. Joseph Gallagher, ed. Walter M. Abbot (New York: Guild Press, 1966). Citing Augustine, *City of God,* book 17, chapter 6, paragraph 2.

5. Bruna Costacurta, "Exégesis y lectura creyente de la Escritura," in *Escritura e Interpretación,* ed. Luis Sánchez Navarro (Madrid: Ediciones Palabra, 2003), 117.

6. *Dei verbum,* §12, citing Augustine, *City of God,* book 17, chapter 6, paragraph 2 (PL 41, 537; CSEL 40, 2:228).

7. *Dei verbum,* §13, citing John Chrysostom, *Homilies on Genesis,* book 3, homily 17, section 1 (PG 53, 134).

The union of the two natures in Christ is an analogy of sacred Scripture. We receive it as a single word insofar as its human expressions are also divine by virtue of the Spirit that inspired them: two natures, unalterable, indivisible, and inseparable, with the distinction of each nature not confused by their union; the property of each is preserved, and they coincide in God's revealed truth.

As for exegesis, it must be critical, but added to the research, we ask ourselves, with regard to the sacredness of the text, to what degree can or should the interpretation be theologically, explicitly open to the premises of faith and the intuition of prayer and praxis. If Scripture is inspired truth, it is a contradiction to limit it to a historical, anthropological, sociological, literary, linguistic, or structural analysis. By narrowing the meaning to what can be gained by the application of the tools of historical criticism, the research encounters its own limitation, bereft of its theological and pastoral meaning. In addition to the literal meaning of the text, the theological and ecclesial impulse of the text is to be sought.[8]

This impulse does not rally in favor of a pious or fundamentalist attitude, nor does it support a naive or pre-scientific reading. Some advances in historical critical methodology have become common heritage in the Church, in particular the awareness of the complex process of formation of which the biblical text is the result.[9] Even so, it would be a mistake to reduce the appreciation of a text to a literal interpretation or to scientific assignations of chronology, or sociological or anthropological hypotheses, or linguistics, or the history of Israel, of interpreters who have not entered into friendship on the level of faith, with the divine author. The two aspects join hands and together offer the interpretation.[10]

Excessive focus on historical critical exegesis to the neglect of ecclesial,

8. Schüssler Fiorenza comments incisively on this point, which can be applied to our programs of teaching Scripture: " . . . the once-reigning hermeneutical division of labor between the exegete who describes what the text *meant* and the pastor/theologian who articulates what the text *means* has been seriously challenged . . .". Cf. Elisabeth Schüssler Fiorenza, "Rethinking the Educational Practices of Biblical Doctoral Studies," in *Transforming Graduate Biblical Education: Ethos and Discipline* ed. E. Schüssler Fiorenza and Kent Harold Richards (Atlanta: Society of Biblical Literature, 2010), 381.

9. Costacurta, "Exégesis y lectura creyente de la Escritura," 118–119.

10. Rudolf Schnackenburg, *Jesus in the Gospels: A Biblical Christology*, trans. O. C. Dean, Jr. (Louisville: Westminster John Knox, 1995), 8–9, comments in this vein: "The real historical Jesus eludes our eyes and is not to be grasped by historical-critical research either. The result of this research . . . is a construct according to procedural methods that are generally employed in historical scholarship but remain totally inadequate for such an unusual figure as Jesus of Nazareth, a figure who can be comprehended only in faith."

personal reflection and additional liturgical and individual prayer inhibits faith, ministry, and personal conversion. Take, for example, the efforts to investigate the person of the historical Jesus. Exegetical research and identification of traditions introduces interpreters into an endless discussion of the history of tradition and redaction. But what the process hopes to achieve is a respect for the purpose of the texts, which is, even in its beginnings, theological reflection in the faith community and in communal friendship with God.[11] I turn again to the analogy of two natures in one person: they are not mutually exclusive, and in their union lies the richness. Given its nature as the Word of God in human language, it would be an oversight on the part of the interpreter to neglect the copulative "and" with respect to either study or prayer.

Our knowledge and appreciation of Scripture is enhanced by the marriage of critical exegesis with the tradition of interpretation of the early Church's theologians and teachers. Alone, the indispensable task of critical investigation does not yield a thorough appreciation and understanding of the sacred text. Settling for what critical research offers is analogous to entering a restaurant, scanning the menu, ordering a main course, and paying the bill, without tasting the food. What about the Spirit that nourishes the interior life and enlivens the message? Approaching the sacred text with an over-confident concentration on critical methodology risks leaving the reader hungry, malnourished, or in a condition like that of the Easter disciples, who saw and reviewed the evidences but did not yet recognize the implications of Jesus' resurrection for the Church and the believer (cf. Luke 24:16; John 20:14; 21:4).

F. Marín Heredia encourages the reader to approach the Bible not as a text or specimen on which to exercise a scientific analysis, but as a vehicle of communication that achieves its full meaning in dialogue. *Dei verbum* emphasizes: "To search out the intention of the sacred writers, attention should be given, among other things, to 'literary forms.'" The dogmatic constitution, in the same paragraph, broadens the horizon and indicates how to achieve this goal:

> Since holy Scripture must be read and interpreted according to the same Spirit by whom it was written, no less serious attention must be given to the content and unity of the whole of Scripture, if the meaning of the sacred texts is to be correctly brought to light. The living tradition of the whole Church must be taken into account along with the harmony which exists between elements of the faith.[12]

11. "The four Gospels draw no 'character pictures' of Jesus but rather faithful-pictures, which in looking back to Jesus establish his historical appearance and his way to the cross and reflect the radiance of the resurrected and glorified one." Schnackenburg, *Jesus in the Gospels*, 13.

12. *Dei verbum*, §12.

To achieve this noble objective and appreciate its complexity, the interpreter assents to the twofold nature of the text. Just as the one who is absent cannot understand one with whom he is at odds, so the mystery of the Bible cannot be properly honored from the stance of an unbeliever, but rather by one who can go beyond the human words in the hope of contacting the Word of God.[13]

The analogy of dialogue is apt, since it reserves space for the divine Word communicated in human language between two interlocutors. How will I value the interior life of the other if it is not revealed and communicated? Or, for my part, if I approach the person with prejudice, mistrust, and suspicion, she may withdraw into herself, and the two of us remain distant strangers. But if I approach her in trust and without prejudice, a free and constructive communication is plausible. The logical implication is that the biggest obstacle in appreciating the beauty and meaning of the text comes from the interior darkness of the interpreter rather than from the penumbra of the text. In applying the analogy to Bible study, a formidable obstacle comes from the pedantry that is sometimes applied in research and exegesis.

When Saint Augustine writes about the relationship between John the Baptist, the voice, and the Messiah, the Word, he affirms that the voice is at the service of the Word; just so, the biblical text exists to put the reader in touch with the Word of God. "The voice without the word strikes the ear but does not reach the heart." The vehicle of the voice carries the word across from one heart to another. "The sound of my voice brings the meaning of the word to you and then passes away. The word which the sound has brought to you is now in your heart, and yet it is still also in mine."[14] Sound, gestures, and words serve as a bridge of communication between two people; with Scripture the words are the bridge between God and the listener. Crossing the bridge of the words on the page brings one to the land of the living and effective Word that takes shape in the believer's life.

"The written letters kill, but the Spirit gives life"[15]

Paul's text, "The written letters kill, but the Spirit gives life" (2 Cor 3:6),[16] refers to the written law, the "letter," of the Old Testament, compared with the inner

13. F. Marín Heredia, *La Biblia, Palabra Profética* (Estella: Verbo Divino, 1992), 270–271.

14. Saint Augustine, Sermon 293, section 3, cited in *The Liturgy of the Hours*, vol. 1 (New York: Catholic Book Publishing Co., 1975), 261.

15. The Bible translation used throughout this chapter is *The New Jerusalem Bible* (Garden City: Doubleday, 1985).

16. Francis of Assisi admonishes his disciples: "The letter kills those who are content to know only the words . . . The letter kills also those religious who do not want to follow the spirit of the divine writing, but are content to know only words and interpret them for others."

law, the spirit, of the new covenant founded in Christ.[17] The understanding of Scripture is not just a matter of the intellect. Paul (cf. 2 Cor 3:12–18) suggests that only Spirit-enabled readers can penetrate the veil of the letters and comprehend their meaning. He expounds the text of Moses and the old covenant in the style of a free, rabbinical commentary (cf. Exod 34:29–35), where, after speaking to God face to face, Moses covered his face with a veil. Paul shows that Christ removes the veil. Only in the light of Jesus Christ, the fullness of revelation, can the true meaning of the sacred books be understood. Those who do not know the spirit of the Messiah can get trapped in study techniques and textual details, and thus, obstructed by the veils over their minds, they are limited by the very words they are reading. The lesson is clear: through the spirit of Christ we share divine life. The Word, when it is incorporated in the reader's life, is understood. As Moses reflected the divine glory in his face after conversing with God, the benefit of our reading Scripture is the reflection of the divine Word in our lives.

The Pauline text is directed to how an intellect may be transformed by Christ, and it specifies how to interpret Scripture. Interwoven into laborious, analytical study is an intuitive reception of faith. Without the exegetical exercise, the Bible risks being reduced to pious platitudes or aphorisms. But in an analogous manner, without faith and insight, by which the spirit of the text speaks for the hearer of today and reflects on the theological sense for the present life of the Church, the contact with the Word of God will be reduced to antiquarianism. The Spirit hovers over the whole enterprise, the intellectual as well as the intuitive faculty of insight and prayer.[18]

Notwithstanding Paul's caution about the letter that can deprive one of life, an essential relationship exists between the written text and the Spirit, and the reader cannot dispense with one or the other. Reading and studying the Bible, without acknowledging the Spirit that inspired the text, is like classifying phonemes and morphemes, without pronouncing the syllable, or without joining

Robert J. Karris, *The Admonitions of Saint Francis: Sources and Meanings* (St. Bonaventure, NY: Franciscan Institute Publications, 2015), 295–296.

17. This argument is developed in similar terms in Rom 2:17–29: see v. 29; 7:6.

18. John Goldingay, *Models for Interpretation of Scripture* (Grand Rapids: Eerdmans, 1995), 188, cites Hays: 2 Cor 3 suggests that "Only readers made competent by the Spirit can throw back the veil and perceive the sense of Scripture; those who have not turned to the Lord who is Spirit are necessarily trapped in the script, with minds hardened and veiled: At the same time, readers who do by the aid of the Spirit discover the glory of God in Scripture are necessarily transformed by the experience." Cf. R. B. Hays, *Echoes of Scripture in the Letters of Paul* (New Haven/London: Yale, 1989), 148.

the syllables to form the words and the sentence and establish meaningful communication. The Spirit is also contacted in the letters and the words of the text.

The Song of Songs is an anthology of love songs. Who would deny that the images, affirmations, and compliments eulogize the adventure of love, with its fascination, allure, setbacks, and uncertainty? This anthology, expressed in passionate and corporeal metaphors, reflects the reciprocal love between God and the chosen people; besides, it is a figure of the covenant and the mutual seeking between God and the individual. The Song resonates with the mystery of the Word of God in human language. The wealth of the text supersedes the scope of historical critical research and opens to a comprehension beyond what investigation alone can achieve. Just as the text is flesh—the "letter" or letters on the page—and spirit—divine inspiration—together, the reader's understanding has incarnational and spiritual dimensions. In research and prayer, the interpreter values various levels of meaning, enters into friendship with God, advances along the path of self-knowledge and conversion, and receives the viaticum for the ministerial life. The images and language challenge the engaged interpreter to chant this love song that becomes incarnate in experience.

One danger is that the critical interpreter impose limits on the text, which by definition is inspired by God and has unlimited scope that embraces both the faithful listener and the professional interpreter. For any inspired reader the very same text may satisfy even as it awakens the appetite for more. In exegesis, a necessary relationship exists between the critical study of a text conditioned by time and the Word of God that transcends time and is valid for all ages.

To sum up, the meaning of the text is belittled to the extent that critical study excludes or does not take into account the theological interest in question. Thus, the critical study may reduce and explain away miracles but it does not remove the mystery. It should be noted, however, that historical criticism cannot be dispensed with, for biblical faith assents to historical facts.[19] In our approach to Scripture, we aim for a delicate balance between the study of the empirical formulation of the argument and the transcendent friendship with God that radiates behind the veil; even with feet firmly planted in the text we expect a revelation of God. An Exodus theologian sketches an image of this delicate and respectful approach to the sacred in the narrative of Moses' approach to the burning bush: "Remove your sandals, for the ground where you stand is holy" (Exod 3:5).

19. Pope Benedict XVI/Joseph Ratzinger, *Jesus of Nazareth* (New York: Penguin Random House, 2007), 11.

"Remove your sandals, for the ground where you stand is holy"

An icon of the human and divine encounter is Moses' bare feet on the ground before the burning bush. The descriptive elements evoke a reality beyond the literal interpretation. One handicap of the exclusive application of historical critical research is the focus on the realistic meaning, a drawback that is especially evident with respect to prophetic and poetic texts that cross the realistic frontiers. Beyond the critical study, the text speaks for itself, and the hearing requires humility on the interpreter's part, the recognition of the limitations of research. The meaning is not found just on the basis of textual analysis and hypothetical reconstructions. Confronted with the narrative, symbolic language and imagery, the reader may feel touched and embraced by the mystery, even without understanding it, or perhaps for that very reason.[20] Ruberval Monteiro da Silva unravels the strong symbols in the narrative of Moses' encounter with God at the burning bush. The image of his bare feet illustrates the fitting attitude of the reader and interpreter of Scripture.

After his abortive attempts to alleviate the problems of slavery in Egypt, and during his forty-year refuge in the land of Midian, Moses' life is intercepted by a unique experience, the narrative details of which are evocative. To relate a profound encounter with God, the theologian shaped a poignant symbol: the feet, where a person touches the ground. "It was necessary for Moses to put his feet on the bare ground, to sense the quality of his own nakedness before a reality that far surpassed his capacity for understanding."[21] The divine voice instructs him: "Come no nearer . . . Take off your sandals, for the place where you are standing is holy ground" (Exod 3:5). In an act of renunciation, Moses removes his sandals. The word *sandal*, Hebrew *na'al*, derives from a verb that means "to close, shut in, tighten, lock up." In Hebrew, to remove the sandals means to open what has been closed, to loose what tightens, or free what imprisons the feet. A mystery captivates Moses: the bush burning without being consumed.

What degree of admiration may motivate an individual to remove his footwear and walk barefoot? Thus, Moses meets God, and opens to a new stage of life and vocation. Removing one's sandals is an act of respect equivalent to stripping the self of what prevents one from entering in skin-to-skin contact with sacred ground. God's presence fascinates and terrifies the individual; it

20. This last sentence is a translation and paraphrase of Ruberval Monteiro da Silva, "La zarza ardiente y el corazón contrito," *Cuadernos Monásticos* 145 (2003): 187–193, at 187.

21. Monteiro da Silva, "La zarza ardiente y el corazón contrito," 189 (translation mine).

attracts even as it keeps one at a distance.[22] I wonder to what extent our application of and fascination with historical critical research of Scripture robs us of the astonishment in the face of the sacred and wholly "other." Do the human words lose their salt, become flat and tasteless, even as they tease the researcher's mind and reason with their linguistic, anthropological, sociological, and psychological implications?

The opposite of the interpreter's removing the sandals would be an investigation of the text devoid of desire for friendship with the God who speaks. An example of how Bible study relates to the life of the Church and challenges the life of the interpreter is the career of Julius Wellhausen (1844–1918), dedicated to teaching the history of the two Testaments. A decisive moment came in 1882 when his personal conviction forced him to resign from his academic chair for reasons of conscience, stating in his letter of resignation:

> I became a theologian because the scientific treatment of the Bible interested me; only gradually did I come to understand that a professor of theology also has the practical task of preparing the students for service in the Protestant Church, and that I am not adequate to this practical task, but that instead despite all caution on my own part I make my hearers unfit for their office. Since then my theological professorship has been weighing heavily on my conscience.[23]

I wonder, how many biblical researchers find themselves in a similar dilemma? Does this impasse exist because we are carried away by the euphoria of the letter to the neglect of the sacred, or because I balk at removing my sandals in the presence of God's Word, as alive and life-giving today as it was yesterday? Might the interpreter who rigorously applies the critical method to the text be like Jacob when he awoke from his dream and exclaimed: "Truly, the Lord is in this place and I did not know!" (Gen 28:16).

Historical Criticism Complemented by Friendship with God

As we approach Scripture, we expect it to offer meaning; if we reach an impasse, the effort may collapse. The child wrestling with mathematics or a frustrated beginner in a language school struggling with the precise meaning of a preposition cries, "This means nothing." Yielding to such a conclusion can block the learning process; this is even truer when it comes to the Word of God. In search

22. Monteiro da Silva, "La zarza ardiente y el corazón contrito," 190–191.

23. Cited in Robert J. Oden Jr., *The Bible Without Theology: The Theological Tradition and Alternatives to It* (San Francisco: Harper and Row, 1987), 20.

of the sacred "otherness"[24] of Scripture, the investigator touches upon the limitations of critical interpretation. In this section I outline some limitations to the exclusive application of historical criticism to the Bible.[25]

One limitation of critical research is the attempt to anchor the text in the past. Critical study derives its conclusions from the hypothetical historical background where texts were formed; researchers strive to unearth the past as accurately as possible in order to discover what the author aimed to communicate in his or her day. To the extent that the research is true to itself, this effort not only situates the word in the past but risks leaving it there. The effort to situate the text in the context of its hypothetical past is both the strength and a limitation of historical critical research.[26]

Moreover, historical criticism presupposes the uniformity of the historical context and tends to limit both narrative and poetry to the criteria of contemporary literary analysis. Prayer and theological reflection disclose an added aspect that enhances the Word. The object of critical study is the analysis of discourse or narrative, and the danger is to divorce oneself from a dimension that transcends the limits of critical study.

Historical criticism favors the diachronic approach insofar as it attempts to place each book of the Bible in its historical context and subdivide it into fragments according to its sources, but in the case of biblical research there exists a recognized unity of the collection, and what is often not taken into account in diachronic analysis is the complement of synchronic analysis. Canonical criticism appreciates the growth of the traditions and the lines of development and perceives, beyond each book, the process of a single book, the Bible, composed of many parts. A limitation of historical criticism is to sound the depths of the texts' origin and isolate them, limiting them to something like a museum piece from the past.[27]

24. In Hebrew, a form of the verb from which is derived the attribute "holy" or "sacred" denotes "to set apart."

25. In the prologue to *Jesus of Nazareth*, 12–14, Pope Benedict XVI/Ratzinger outlines some of these.

26. Pope Benedict XVI/Ratzinger, *Jesus of Nazareth*, 12–13.

27. "The 'canonical' approach . . . proceeds from the perception that the historical-critical method experiences at times considerable difficulty in arriving, in its conclusions, at a truly theological level. It aims to carry out the theological task of interpretation more successfully by beginning from within an explicit framework of faith: the Bible as a whole. To achieve this, it interprets each biblical text in the light of the canon of Scriptures, that is to say, of the Bible as received as the norm of faith by a community of believers. It seeks to situate each text within the single plan of God, the goal being to arrive at a presentation of Scripture truly valid for our

An example from the prophets reveals another limitation of the rigorous application of historical critical research. The literary critic of the Bible is urged to take into account the historical referent and context. However, texts that are largely poetry assume a metaphorical and meta-historical referent that thwarts direct access to historical roots. This fact makes it difficult to arrive at a definitive historical application of texts that refer, for example, to the call of the prophet (for example, Isa 6:1–13; Jer 1:4–10), to Hosea's challenging marriage (1:1–3), the "Servant of the Lord" texts (Isa 42:1–4; 49:1–6; 50:4–9; 52:13–53:12), the prophetic oracle of Jerusalem at the end of time (cf. Isa 60 and 62; Zech 14:1–21), and texts of an eschatological or apocalyptic genre. Such compositions came to light in a particular time and social context, and their study finally admits their trans-historical, theological motivation and dimension.

For example, Genesis describes Jacob's deathbed farewell to his twelve sons (Gen 49:8–10). The patriarch's prophetic discourse tells the future of his descendants; in particular, he addresses Judah, the father of the homonymous tribe from which the Messiah will be born. This prophecy, perhaps dating to the time of Isaiah (eighth–seventh century BC), extols the royal superiority of Judah, like a lion, over the other tribes. The fragment alludes to the Davidic monarchy in which resides the scepter of God's anointed, that will usher in the long-awaited salvation when the ideal king rules over all peoples. Several contexts are attributed to the text: the historical when, in all likelihood, it was pronounced; the literary context of Genesis; and its present context for the Jewish or Christian audience, who applies the prophecy to the Messiah, yet awaited or already come and reigning in the Church. Critical research risks confining this text to its historical or literary setting, without taking into account its depth of meaning for the contemporary reader.

Another limitation of the exclusive application of historical criticism is the study of prophetic texts that, besides being set in a particular time, are evocative in their application, whence comes their fruitfulness for the interpreter. The editors of these oracles presumed a message beyond what they knew; they were not aware of the breadth of implications of their phrases, words, and images that escape the rigor of historical and literary investigation, and the premise is that any interpretation may elicit a deeper understanding of what the prophets themselves communicated rather than an allegory of their

time. The method, rather than a substitute for historical criticism, complements it." Pontifical Biblical Commission, *The Interpretation of the Bible in the Church* (March 18, 1994) (London: SCM Press, 1995), §I.C.1, p. 27.

words.[28] Relying on historical criticism, the interpretation sinks roots in the formulation of texts conditioned by the historic background when the prophets came to light. The same spirit who inspires it moves the intuitive interpreter who is open to the actualization of the prophecy.

The interpretation of parabolic discourse in both Testaments suffers from the limitations of historical critical research. In its original state the prophetic pantomime, like Isaiah walking naked and barefoot for three years as a prophetic sign for the people (Isa 6:1–6), or Jeremiah breaking the potter's vessel (Jer 19:1–13), or the parables in the Old and New Testament, was addressed to specific audiences; but the discourse lost its referent when applied to successive generations in diverse social or ecclesial contexts. Because it is Scripture, the recipient in succeeding generations legitimately applies the parable both to the time of the prophet, to that of the Messiah, to that of the community of the evangelist or editorial school, and to the contemporary generation. The fact that parables have a historical referent and a context makes it necessary to apply the principles of critical research to their analysis, but mere study does not exhaust the interpretative possibilities that metaphorical language implies. As Scripture, the text that addressed yesterday's generation enters into dialogue with that of today. The Holy Spirit, inspirer of biblical texts, gives impetus to the application of the discourse beyond the original context in ways that human authors could not have guessed.[29]

The application of the historical critical method is necessary because the biblical text is language, but research itself is not enough to sound the depths of Scripture, which in itself does not necessarily challenge and question the reader, especially if he or she does not recognize the inspired character of the Word. It remains an engraved or printed codex that requires analysis and research that may content itself with the archaeology of the Scriptures. Prayer, under the inspiration of the same Spirit that breathes in the text, transforms a plain page into *sacra pagina*. Conversely, research that ignores the inspiration faces the danger of turning sacred script—whether it is a magnificent piece of literature like the Song of Songs, the philosophical musing of Job, the classical composition of Hebrews or the Gospel of John—into prosaic literature.

Last but not least, the reader's knowledge, background, and capacity may limit the interpretation, with the result that the theological, trans-historical dimension of Scripture may escape scientific artifice. Any attempt to ascertain the past finally hits the wall of hypothesis. Even when scientific theory achieves

28. Goldingay, *Models for Interpretation of Scripture*, 186–187.
29. Goldingay, *Models for Interpretation of Scripture*, 187.

a high degree of probability, it is to the researcher's advantage to maintain a healthy mistrust of what might seem to be airtight conclusions. The reader uses every faculty at his or her disposal to interpret the text and get in touch with Scripture; after all, the aim of interpretation is to leave behind the methods and theories and finally find oneself alone with the author—and the Author (in capital letters)![30] In the image drawn by the psalmist, it is pointless to trust in the chariots of wit or in the cavalry of exegetical methodology; the real motive for trust in biblical interpretation is friendship with the Lord (cf. Ps 147:10–11): "Some call on chariots, some on horses, but we on the name of Yahweh our God" (Ps 20:8).

To overcome the limitations of the interpreter's liability, *Dei verbum*, citing Ambrose of Milan, exhorts us: "And let them remember that prayer should accompany the reading of sacred Scripture, so that God and man may talk together; for 'we speak to Him when we pray; we hear Him when we read the divine sayings'."[31] In a similar vein, Jerome affirms in a letter to Eustochium, "Do you pray? You speak to the Bridegroom. Do you read? He speaks to you."[32] In prayer we receive what is divine; there would be no reason to consider it divine if we could obtain it through our own resources. Rather, it would be considered a mere human word, fraught with the limitations of language.

Precaution

As a precaution to critical biblical research and interpretation that dispense with prayer and friendship with God, take the analogy of architecture. We approach a splendid building and are amazed at the elegance of the facade. We

30. Benjamin Jowett, "On the Interpretation of Scripture," in *Essays and Reviews*, by F. Temple, et al. (London: Longman, 1860), 466: "The true use of interpretation is to get rid of interpretation, and leave us alone with the author."

31. *Dei verbum,* §25, citing Saint Ambrose, *On the Duties of Ministers*, book 1, chapter 20, section 88 (PL l6, 50). Saint Augustine writes succinctly, "Pray that you may understand." On Christian Doctrine, in NPNF 2, ed. Philip Schaff (Peabody: Hendrickson, 1887/2004), book 3, chapter 37, section 56. In this context, Augustine writes of the need for an intellectual as well as a devout approach to sacred Scripture: "Students of these venerable documents ought to be counselled not only to make themselves acquainted with the forms of expression ordinarily used in Scripture, to observe them carefully, and to remember them accurately, but also, what is especially and before all things necessary, to pray that they may understand them." Augustine takes his inspiration from Prov 2:6, which speaks of God alone who is the giver of even the desire for knowledge, if it is wedded to faith: "For Yahweh himself is giver of wisdom, from his mouth issue knowledge and understanding."

32. Saint Jerome, *Letter* 22, 25, trans. W. H. Fremantle, NPNF 6, ed. Philip Schaff (Peabody: Hendrickson, 1893/2004).

survey the outside of the building and admire the beauty, utility, and architectural genius. Once inside, the serene interior radiates warmth and peace. Investigating the biblical text without praying stands in admiration of the calligraphy and the tools used to craft it, without contacting the Author and enjoying the marvelous truth and sublime mystery the parchment holds. The interpreter insistently knocks on the door of the text; when it finally opens, suddenly he or she realizes that all the while he was "confined" outside, and now is invited to enter and enjoy the beauty and elegance of the whole.

Deacon Ephrem the Syrian asks:

> Lord, who can comprehend even one of your words? We lose more of it than we grasp, like those who drink from a living spring. For God's Word offers different facets according to the capacity of the listener, and the Lord has portrayed his message in many colors, so that whoever gazes upon it can see in it what suits him. Within it he has buried manifold treasures so that each of us might grow right in seeking them out.[33]

Ephrem warns the reader of the danger of contenting oneself with a single interpretation. The exegete discovers treasures that arouse interest, but, of many possibilities found on the sacred page, choosing a single interpretation would result a poor selection of all that is offered. What about when our harvest in the field of the Word seems insignificant? Let us avoid concluding that Scripture itself is poor and sterile, but rather give thanks for all the wealth it encloses.

> A thirsty man is happy when he is drinking, and he is not depressed because he cannot exhaust the spring. So let this spring quench your thirst, and not your thirst the spring. For if you can satisfy your thirst without exhausting the spring, then when you thirst again you can drink from it once more; but if when your thirst is sated the spring is also dried up, then your victory would turn to your own harm.[34]

When it comes to seeking advice about how to access Scripture, it is best to appeal to wisdom. In the inaugural prayer of his reign, Solomon asked for a *leb šômea'*, a listening heart (1 Kgs 3:6–15; cf. v. 9), which Jerome translated as *cor docile*; the expression refers to a person who has the capacity to listen. In Sirach, Wisdom eulogizes herself: "They who eat me will hunger for more, they who drink me will thirst for more" (Sir 24:21).[35] Here we pose the analogy

33. Saint Ephrem, deacon, *On the Diatessaron*, chapter 1, sections 18–19 (SC 121, 52–53), cited in *The Liturgy of the Hours*, vol. 3 (New York: Catholic Book Publishing Co., 1975), pp. 199–200.

34. Saint Efrem, *On the Diatessaron*, 1.18–19.

35. Sir 24, by its content, is the high point of the book and the centerpiece for a theology

of the regulation of the collection of manna (cf. Exod 16:16–22). God legislated that only a daily ration of manna was to be collected, with a double portion for the sixth day. The reader of the Bible is cautioned against avarice and gluttony, presuming to take and store up more than what one needs for a day at a time, with the exception of the Sabbath ration. Likewise, according to the regulation of the harvest, the reaper is forbidden to glean to the very edges of the field or gather the leavings of the harvest; one is not to strip the vineyard bare or gather every last grape or olive from the vineyard or tree. Something is always left for the poor and migrant (Lev 19:9–10; 23:22; Deut 24:19–21).

Henri de Lubac presents an analogy for the study and understanding of Scripture:

> The spirit that strives to "comprehend" [God's Word] is not like that of the miser who heaps an increasing quantity of gold, a sum of truths. Neither does he resemble the artist who time and again returns to a sketch to perfect it, until he finally rests in the aesthetic enjoyment of his art. It is rather like the swimmer who, to stay afloat in the surf, advances in the ocean, and with each stroke has to reject one wave in favor of the next. He repeatedly rejects the representations that change at any moment, knowing full well that he is drawn by them, but holding on to them would be death.[36]

It is convenient for the interpreter to cultivate a healthy distrust of one's own abilities and skills and be wary of clinging too closely to one's own prejudices, presumptions, and preconceived conclusions. The truth of the sacred text lies beyond the reach of arguments and methods; it is in the life of God with his people. The rigor of research is applied, yet with healthy mistrust of any system that ignores the Spirit that blows around, in, through, and in spite of the letter. What is necessary is love, veneration of the inspired Word, and a healthy knowledge of one's own motivations and needs.

Venerate the Word

To what end do we teach and interpret sacred Scripture? William of Saint-Thierry comments: "For reading serves the purpose of the intention with which it is done. If the reader truly seeks God in his reading, everything that he reads tends to promote that end, making the mind surrender in the course of the reading and bring all that is understood into Christ's service."[37] William

of wisdom.

36. Henri de Lubac, *Por los caminos de Dios* (Madrid: Ediciones Encuentro, 1993), 94 (translation mine).

37. William of Saint Thierry, *The Golden Epistle: A Letter to the Brethren at Mont Dieu*,

draws the analogy of casual acquaintance and true friendship. There is a huge difference between, on the one hand, attentive study and reading, as if entertaining a passing guest, and, on the other hand, deep, heartfelt friendship.[38]

Because it is God's Word, the Scriptures are polyvalent, and they speak in unpredictable ways. We relate to them not only with antiquarian interest, using our reason to decipher and analyze an artifact, but as a people in search of friendship with God. The inspiration of the text is complemented by the Spirit's action in the life of the reading public. Rather than the intellectual mastery or excellence of the method, friendship with God and prayer has the final word when it comes to the eloquence of the text. Thus, interpreters may be guilty of forcing understanding or wanting to have the last word. Historical critical research can give rise to the sin of gluttony when one tries to exhaust the possibilities and amass all meaning with reference to the composition. But Scripture is not restricted to what the scientific interpreter can discover. After all, it is not in the results of the research where lasting happiness is to be found, but in the fruits of the Spirit translated in the interpreter's life. The text comes to life and acquires meaning and vitality in the friendly reader.

Conclusion to Part One

I have addressed the theme of the synergy between biblical interpretation and friendship with God, as cultivated in prayer. As Scripture exists for the faith formation of God's people and of the individual, the friendship is not constrained by a critical study of the past, but rather seeks an expression, a resonance of the Word of God in today's ecclesial life, as well as a personal relationship that at best is expressed in conversion, loving service, and prayer. The marriage between historical critical research and prayerful reading promotes a theological interpretation of the Bible based on faith without renouncing the seriousness of scientific interest. The twofold nature of Scripture calls for an approach that transcends the methods of interpretation and relates us to its divine author. Like Moses before the burning bush, it is prudent to approach barefoot, to complement the interpretive enterprise with prayer, to overcome the limitations inherent in any method of research and the limitation of the

trans. Theodore Berkeley, *The Works of William of St. Thierry*, Cistercian Fathers 12 (Spencer, MA: Cistercian Publications, 1971), book 1, paragraph 124, p. 52. In Migne's *Patrologia Latina*, volume 184, this would be book 1, paragraph 31.

38. William of Saint Thierry, *The Golden Epistle*, 1.121. Further on, William writes, "The reading should also stimulate the feelings and give rise to prayer, which should interrupt your reading: an interruption which should not so much hamper the reading as restore to it a mind ever more purified for understanding" (1.123).

interpreter, as well as to respect the mystery of divinely inspired Scripture. Thus, the sacred text grows as it is read and interpreted.

In conclusion to this first part, I note an analogy of the interpreter's task that is complemented by friendship with the Word of God. What did the Hebrews eat in the desert? Naturalists identify this food scientifically, while generations within the biblical tradition celebrate what wondrous food comes from God (Ps 78:25; 105:40; Wis 16:20–21, 25–26). The very text of Exodus reveals the tension (Exod 16:14–16): "When the layer of dew lifted, there on the surface of the desert was something fine and granular, as fine as hoarfrost on the ground. As soon as the Israelites saw this, they said to one another, 'What is that?' [Hebrew, *mân hû'* = manna], not knowing what it was." The interpreter, faced with the letter inscribed on the parchment, asks, what is this? Even as he spells the letters of the word, *m-a-n-n-a*, he writes "the food which Yahweh has given you to eat." In this text, the exegete and the interpreter join hands. The mute letter on the page intrigues the exegete who looks for clarity, even as it questions the meaning. One asks, what is manna? The scientific analysis of the text concludes "something fine and granular, as fine as hoarfrost on the ground," and the same theologian expounds the truth: manna, "the food which Yahweh has given you to eat." Between these two readings, the scientific and the theological, stands the expression that asks and responds at the same time, "What is this . . . manna?"[39]

Part Two: *Lectio* Seminar

Two Wings of Pedagogy

We have two wings with which to approach the Bible, academic study and prayer. A friend of God who neglects one or the other wing will only with difficulty and grace soar to the heights of the divine Word in human syntax. For a number of years in Scripture study in many theological faculties, the focus has been on the history and explanation of the text on historical, sociological, and cultural grounds—with hardly a head bow to the linguistic; the theological questions are often left to be ironed out by the systematic, moral, liturgical, and pastoral faculties. The result of such an emphasis can be to divorce the student from the comprehensiveness of the interpretative enterprise, as if the personal relationship with the text were somehow less important. But the two wings fly as one: the knowledge that results from study is connected to our personal lives in the Church; the two wings together give equilibrium to the flight.

39. An example from Paul Beauchamp, "La lettre: méthodes et interprétation," in *Le récit, la lettre et le corps: Essais bibliques* (Paris: Les éditions du Cerf, 1992), 31.

The Challenge of Literacy in a Fast-Moving Age

I begin with a relatively simple, yet controversial theme: the intellectual formation of our students, their ability to read, and their facility with the cybernetic world of information.[40] We have a rich tradition to assimilate: the Bible, the development of theology and the Church in the first seven centuries, and the evolution of theology in its various branches, systematic, sacramental, moral, and pastoral. Have we arrived at an age when the challenge of assimilation is faced with the tremendous sophistication and complexity of our theological tradition? Yes, to a certain extent. But in some circles, even persons with little formal intellectual formation are able to enter Scripture with understanding, appreciation, and even pleasure.

We are challenged in academic formation programs to address what has been perceived as an imbalance between intellectual and human formation. We have access to fine libraries, both traditional and digital, accredited professors, and bibliographic material, so adequate resources are not the issue. Rather, the challenge is that, for fault of practice or due to negative experiences, the textbook, the classroom, the library, the professor, and Google operate in one area of life, and personal and spiritual formation occupies another space. Here I address the faculty of reading.

In a cultural climate where communication is immediate and brief, many students do not know that they actually enjoy reading. To put it another way, the reading of many students before entering theology was a matter of homework, utility, or surfing the net. How to approach a poetic or philosophic text, the value of which resides in its own beauty, train of thought, or simply in its approximation to the truth?

When a person enters the biblical world, he or she may experience something fascinating; he may be charmed by the personalities and become the companion of David, Esther, Daniel, Simon Peter, Paul, the Magdalene, the beloved disciple; he may become enthralled with new ways of looking at law and mercy, love and anger, wisdom and fear of the Lord. The discovery of the wealth of the Bible does not begin with the creation stories of Genesis, but with an experience analogous to that of Abraham, Moses, David, or a disciple of Jesus. This is an experience more Cartesian than that of Descartes, whose "Cogito, ergo sum" represents an attempt to confirm his existence by means of the reflective consciousness. In reference to the Bible and *lectio divina*, a

40. This reflection was inspired by Bernardo Bonowitz, *Apto a Ganhar as Almas: Direção espiritual no contexto monástico* (Juiz de Fora: Edições Subiaco, 2014), 132–134.

similar equation may inspire a surge of admiration and joy: I think, I reflect, I read, I understand, I grow—therefore, I am . . . and more than I ever imagined myself to be.

Such a discovery will not come just by means of a systematic reading of the early Church theologians. Given the basis of a friendship with Jesus nourished by contact with Scripture, and given the practical interest in our education faculties, I offer a modest recommendation as to the curriculum of Scripture study starting with the propaedeutic level: Read the Bible, with ample examples that illustrate salient features in chronology, history, archeology, institutions, customs, and, to an elemental extent, linguistic. But, as we read the Bible and appreciate its vast diversity, may we learn also to enjoy our reading.[41]

Enjoy Reading

To cultivate reading enjoyment, add more ingredients to the recipe, taking the cue from Jesus who put "new wine into fresh wineskins" (Matt 9:17). In this case, the fresh wineskins would be the hearts of the disciples. The new wine? A book of poetry by Walt Whitman; historical fiction by Margaret Mitchell, Stephen Crane, Mark Twain, Ann Rinaldi; the social criticism in the novels of Walker Percy, or a play by Tennessee Williams; a classic moral piece by F. Scott Fitzgerald, Graham Greene, or John Steinbeck; the garlic and onions of Charles Dickens, Thomas Hardy, or Mario Vargas Llosa.

Inseparable from this enterprise is to accompany the students as they read. Besides introducing them to the delight of the classics in spirituality and the big names of philosophy and theology, accompany them in their reading of English and world literature; relive what it feels like to mount the donkey and battle windmills alongside Don Quixote, guided by Miguel de Cervantes, or descend into the bowels of the inferno with Dante Alighieri. Literature is the companion of the mind and the imagination. But the heart of the disciple needs a true-to-life companion to inspire him and share the whimsy. And if the dean of studies questions this procedure of giving a space to "profane" reading, let him recall

41. With regard to this point, I concur with a critique Elisabeth Schüssler Fiorenza made of doctoral biblical education, which to some degree is also reflected in our seminaries, where the biblical curriculum shows a preference for the philological-historical or exegetical paradigm. Students are left with the impression that the aim and requirement of Bible study is the acquisition and control of factual and disciplinary knowledge that can be tested in exams. Our challenge is to revise our teaching the Bible so that it not only serves the academic interests of acquisition of knowledge and technique but also lets its effects be felt in personal conversion and the pastoral ministry. Cf. Elisabeth Schüssler Fiorenza, "Rethinking the Educational Practices of Biblical Doctoral Studies," 379–380.

the wise scribe in the gospel who "brings out from his storeroom new things as well as old" (Matt 13:52). With time the young person just might develop a taste for spiritual reading, the Bible, and even patristics. One hopes to awaken in him sensitivity to plot, characterization, symbolic language, the poetry of the psalms, and themes that will enrich their *lectio*. This reading exercise can be done in seminar fashion, as it was done in the early Jewish religious culture.

Midrash: Rereading and Interpreting Texts for a New Generation

The literary genre of midrash[42] appears in the Old Testament from the time that Israel began to reflect on her traditions. Recall the historical and legislative texts that were spawned in the time of the exile and after; particularly in the Persian era, parts of the Torah and the prophetic books were assuming a form similar to the canonical form of today. Midrash is a rereading of Scripture in its new context. In no way does it pretend to impose the literal sense of the text; rather, as a meditation on the sacred text, *lectio* looks toward the edification of the faithful. It may appear as an imaginative reconstruction of a previous scene or episode, always with the objective of formulating a practical application for the contemporary generation of hearers or readers. Thus, a precept or an episode may be recounted not in terms of its historical context, but in order to shed light and orientation for the new reading public.[43]

Some well-known examples of midrash are, in the Pentateuch, the sacerdotal amplifications of the creation and the flood, some episodes in the lives of the patriarchs, the exodus, and the covenant. In comparison with the older tradition—referred to as the "Yahwist"—these texts demonstrate the intention of the priestly school to elaborate homiletic amplifications of the tradition for a later, postexilic generation. A good example is the books of Chronicles, where the theologian reorganizes the material from the books of Samuel and Kings according to his contemporary theological concepts. Also, the book of

42. In Hebrew, the term *midrāš* (from the verb *drš*, "examine," "interpret") refers to the rabbinic exegesis of Scripture. The midrash may take the form of a commentary that interprets a sacred text verse by verse, but its more customary application refers to an edifying paraphrase, amplified and enriched by details, sometimes legendary or even fantastic, as in the case of haggadic midrash; it is a written account of sermons or of homilies pronounced in the synagogues or Sabbath schools or during the feasts, and at times inspired by important events in public or private life—war, famine, circumcision, marriage, funerals. In relation to the legal texts, the midrash aims to define their application to daily life, or to adapt practical directives for the current generation (halachic midrash).

43. João E. M. Terra, *Lectio Divina: Meditação, oração e contemplação da Palavra de Deus* (São Paulo: Ave Maria, 2009), 116–117. Chapter III, "A Lectio Divina no judaísmo," illustrates the concept of midrash and lectio (105–150).

Wisdom recasts the exodus and the plagues of Egypt and freely amplifies them, adding, suppressing, and adapting the happenings according to his contemporary theological or literary interests. The sage's description of manna in the wilderness is famous:

> How differently with your people! You gave them the food of angels, from heaven untiringly providing them bread already prepared, containing every delight to satisfy every taste. And the substance you gave showed your sweetness towards your children, for, conforming to the taste of whoever ate it, it transformed itself into what each eater wished. (Wis 16:20–21)[44]

Ezekiel 16 rereads the history of Israel in allegorical form with an interest in the prophet's contemporary generation in exile. Isaiah 60–62 recasts and adapts the discourses of Isaiah 40–55, applying them in view of the renewed, practical application to Jerusalem after the exile. Sirach 24 is based on Proverbs 8 (see vv. 22–23), especially in its identification of law with wisdom.[45]

The objective of a midrashic rereading and interpretation is to apply the biblical text to the ears of society today. The rabbinical midrash also provides a rereading of the Old Testament, a homiletic commentary, that aims to update the event or the law, and offers practical applications for the contemporary generation. Often it appears as a free rendition or paraphrase that amplifies Scripture with new or legendary facts. This process does not stop with the Hebrew Bible. Sayings, traditions, and the memory of Jesus were simmering in oriental Mediterranean communities in the first century, and catechetical communities like those of Mark, Matthew, and Luke applied these traditions in their own ways to their communities.

The midrash is the result of a Scripture reading where the reader transfers and applies the values of traditional texts to the present life. To this end, the interpreter clarifies Scripture to evoke, beyond the literal meaning of the words, a meaning in relation to the problems and challenges of his own time. What comes to mind is the application of the circumcision and dietary prescriptions as they are presented in the New Testament. What was Jesus' attitude in the

44. The so-called "historical" psalms (72, 105, 106), Sir 44–50, and Wis 16–19 present midrashic reinterpretations of the past.

45. A number of examples of the midrashic genre are noted by Terra, 117–118. Many scholars follow Michael Fishbane in tracing the origins of rabbinic midrash to these types of a biblical text interpreting itself or another biblical text. According to this argument, Deuteronomy may be seen as a form of midrash on the exodus and wilderness traditions; certain prophets may be seen as doing midrash on the laws of the Torah; and some New Testament writings are based on a rereading of traditional texts from the Old Testament. Michael Fishbane, *Biblical Interpretation in Ancient Israel* (Oxford: Clarendon, 1985).

face of pharisaic criticism of the disciples eating with unwashed hands (Mark 7:1–23; par., Matt 15:1–20)? The way the controversy is related, we perceive a situation in the Matthean and Markan communities that was challenged with interpreting the traditional legal texts and applying them to a new generation of non-Jewish believers. Against the narrow, legalistic, and external practices in matters of purification, external worship, and observance of the commandments, Jesus promotes the true moral intent of the divine law (vv. 8–13).[46]

The principal aim of midrash is to maintain contact between Scripture and the present life of the hearer or reader. The Word of the living God runs the risk of becoming a dead letter when one limits it to its historical sense, dispensing from the contemporary situation in which it is proclaimed. Midrash reinterprets Scripture for the present generation of readers, with a view to maintaining their quality of friendship with God.

Collegial Lectio *Rebuilds an Identity in Nehemiah*

The book of Nehemiah narrates the exuberant collegial *lectio divina* on the day of the consecration of the new temple (Neh 8).[47] The scene recalls a dark period of history, where the people had lost the sense of the transcendence of their life; it celebrates a key moment in the effort to unify the returnees from Babylon captivity. For the first time after the exile, Israel gathered as a people, celebrated the liturgy of the Word, and participated in a communion rite. The ceremony revived the consciousness of the covenant, the foundation of Israel's life. What remained of the Jewish people with their land annexed to the Persian empire, the monarchy annulled, rebuilding the temple delayed, and squatters occupying the properties of the exiles? One remaining institution would unify God's people: the law, transmitted by Moses. To mark the covenant renewal and the birth of Judaism, the priest Ezra solemnly proclaimed this law, and the people agreed to its conditions. Even more important than city fortifications, "rejoicing in the Lord must be your strength," and on this basis faithful hearers of the Word would anticipate the future with renewed hope. In order for God's

46. Acts 15 is a record of the Apostolic Council in Jerusalem. The growth of the Church among the gentiles raised a question of principle that had to be resolved before the gospel could expand freely beyond its Jewish nucleus. Can gentiles be allowed to join the Church direct from the pagan world, or do they only have access via a prior attachment to the synagogue and its ancestral prescriptions, including circumcision? This example is not properly what we identify as an outcome of *lectio*, but it does illustrate the basic issue related to that of the rereading and reinterpretation of sacred texts.

47. The first reading for the third Sunday in Ordinary Time (year C): Neh 8:2–4a, 5–6, 8–10.

people to rebuild among the ruins, they initiated a formation program based on attention to the Word of God. Thus, hearing this Word, Nehemiah's assembly was disappointed, on account of the tremendous distance that separated their lives from the truth of the divine Word. Ezra's advice to those who led the assembly? "Do not be mournful, do not weep. . . . You may go; eat what is rich, drink what is sweet and send a helping to the man who has nothing prepared. For today is sacred to our Lord" (Neh 8:9–10).

The responsorial psalm to this lectionary reading with its antiphon (Ps. 18) extols *lectio divina*: "You have, Lord, the words of eternal life," a verse from the Gospel of John, in the context of the multiplication of the loaves and Jesus' discourse on the bread of life. Many disciples, shocked at Jesus' words, had abandoned him, so he asked those who remained, "Do you want to go away too?" to which Simon Peter replied, "Lord, to whom shall we go? You have the message of eternal life" (John 6:67–68). The benefits of friendship with the eternal Word? The psalmist chants a litany in praise of *lectio*:

> Perfect the Word, comforting the soul;
> immutable the Word, instructing to the simple;
> reliable the Word, rejoicing the heart;
> luminous the Word, lighting the way. (Ps 19:7–8)

Who would refuse comfort, wisdom, joy, and light?

Curriculum Concerns: The Priest and the Bible

In a chapter entitled "Curricular Dreams," Dale Martin recommends that we learn from the early Christian tradition how to read Scripture.

> Augustine . . . prayed Scripture, but in a dialogical sense of prayer. He did appropriate its voice as his own, yet he also heard in its text the voice of God speaking directly to him. Simply the constancy with which many monks recited, sang, and heard Scripture meant that the words, stories, and images of Scripture came to saturate their environments and their bodies. In the early fifth century, for instance, Cassian quotes Abbot Nesteros who insists that Scripture "ought to be constantly poured into our ears or should ever proceed from our lips . . . And so it will come to pass that not only every purpose and thought of your heart, but also the wanderings and rovings of your imagination will become to you a holy and unceasing pondering of the Divine law."[48]

48. Dale B. Martin, *Pedagogy of the Bible: An Analysis and Proposal* (Louisville/London: Westminster John Knox, 2008), 99; cited by Greer in James L. Kugel and Roland A. Greer, *Early Biblical Interpretation* (Philadelphia: Westminster, 1986), 191. The quotation is from Cassian's *Conferences* 14, chapter 13.

With such a practice, the Word of God becomes the "background music" in a person's life, tempering, in a sense filtering, the many other voices that reach us and can perturb our interior life. God's Word has a cleansing effect on the conscience. John Cassian affirms that Scripture will so purify the memory that the moral and spiritual life will be leavened by contact with the Word of God. In his *Conferences*, Abbot Moses addresses the benefits of *lectio*: "And so daily and hourly turning up the ground of our heart with the gospel plough, i.e., the constant recollection of the Lord's cross, we shall manage to stamp out or extirpate from our hearts the lairs of noxious beasts and the lurking places of poisonous serpents."[49]

Israel's priests and scribes proclaimed and studied the Word in the assembly. What we know as the Old Testament, preserved in the synagogues, was read and meditated during the great feasts and in the Sabbath liturgy. In a sense, this refers to the practice of *lectio collegialis*, as the majority of the hearers did not read, nor did they have access to the biblical manuscripts. The practice of *lectio divina* sinks its roots in this practice. In his Gospel, Luke records Jesus' visit to the Nazareth synagogue (Luke 4:16–21, where he cites a free version of Isa 61:1–2):

> [Jesus] came to Nazareth where he had been brought up, and went into the synagogue on the Sabbath day as he usually did. He stood up to read . . . Once he finished, he rolled up the scroll, gave it back to the assistant and sat down. . . . Then he began to speak to them, "This text is being fulfilled today even while you are listening." (Luke 4:16–21)

This *lectio* places the community in direct contact with the Word of God.

This happened also when Jesus resurrected accompanied the disciples to Emmaus; as he rehearsed the Scriptures that referred to him, the disciples' hearts burned within them. Such is the effect of *lectio*: to warm the heart by contact with God's Word. In his last instruction to the apostles, before the Ascension, Jesus reveals the messianic meaning of all the Scriptures (Luke 24:44–48), identifying himself as the key to their interpretation. What would happen if we, in our interpretations of the Old Testament, interpreted the text with the same freedom as Jesus in the Gospels?

The Pontifical Biblical Commission, in the document *Interpretation of the Bible in the Church*, addresses the practice of *lectio* and promotes it both for the individual and the community.

49. John Cassian, *Conferences*, in NPNF 11, ed. Philip Schaff (Grand Rapids: Eerdmans, 1898/1973), conference 1, chapter 22, p. 306.

> The end in view is to create and nourish "an efficacious and constant love" of Sacred Scripture, source of the interior life and of apostolic fruitfulness (EnchBib, 591 and 567), also to promote a better understanding of the liturgy and to assure the Bible a more important place in theological studies and in prayer.[50]

John Paul II, in the apostolic exhortation *Pastores dabo vobis*, anticipated this statement when he wrote of the priest, emphasizing values that apply to any minister of the Word of God, who

> ought first of all to develop a great personal familiarity with the Word of God. Knowledge of its linguistic or exegetical aspects, though certainly necessary, is not enough. He needs to approach the Word with a docile and prayerful heart so that it may deeply penetrate his thoughts and feelings and bring about a new outlook in him—"the mind of Christ" (1 Cor 2:16)—such that his words and his choices and attitudes may become ever more a reflection, a proclamation and a witness to the Gospel.[51]

Through contact with God's Word, the minister becomes the Lord's disciple, "aware that the words of his ministry are not 'his,' but those of the One who sent him. He is not the master of the Word, but its servant."[52]

Another strong voice in the promotion of *lectio divina*, Carlo Maria Martini, writing on the importance of the Bible in the soul of the Church and for the formation of the faithful, encourages an encounter with the Lord through contact with the Bible, promoting the biblical text as a companion for people, to promote knowledge and friendship with the Lord, as a benefit of contact with the Word. "The purpose of the biblical apostolate in all its forms is not to create biblical experts, but men and women of prayer who let the Bible lead them to knowledge of the Lord who calls them in the real situation of their lives, here and now."[53] As we navigate the sea of Bible history and linguistics, let us fix our eyes and trust on the Spirit in whom we read and understand God's Word.

Pope Benedict XVI, in an audience with the episcopal conference of Switzerland (November 7, 2006), animated priests and ministers of the faith to receive a solid training in theology so as to impart knowledge and "inculcate in

50. Pontifical Biblical Commission, *Interpretation of the Bible in the Church* (March 18, 1994), §IV.C.2.

51. Pope John Paul II, *Pastores dabo vobis* (March 15, 1992) (Washington, DC: United States Catholic Conference, 1992), §26.

52. Pope John Paul II, *Pastores dabo vobis*, §26.

53. Cardinal Carlo Maria Martini, "He Explained the Scripture to Us," Address to the 43rd Plenary Assembly of the Italian Bishops' Conference in May 1997, trans. Henry Wansbrough, *Bulletin Dei Verbum* 47, no. 2 (1998): 4–10, at 7.

students an intelligent faith so that faith becomes intelligence and intelligence, faith."[54]

On this occasion Pope Benedict extolled the notable advances that have been made in exegesis, how we know about the development of texts, hypothesize about sources, and know what words meant in their anthropological context, and he commented, "But we are increasingly seeing that if historical and critical exegesis remains solely historical and critical, it refers the Word to the past, it makes it a Word of those times, a Word which basically says nothing to us at all." Benedict laments that we encounter the Word as "fragmented, precisely because it is broken up into a multitude of different sources." He points out that, in accord with the conciliar document *Dei verbum*, "Scripture, which must consequently be interpreted according to historical methods, should also be read in its unity and must be read within the living community of the Church." He desires that theologians approach the Bible in accordance with the guidelines of *Dei verbum*: "May they experience the inner unity of Scripture—something that today is helped by 'canonical exegesis' . . . —and then make a spiritual interpretation of it that is not externally edifying but rather an inner immersion in the presence of the Word." To achieve this, it would be important to provide an introduction to "Scripture as an up-to-date Word of God beside, with, and in historical-critical exegesis." This presents a challenge to our faculties and formation programs, to foster a true encounter with Scripture in the context of the faith of the Church. Such an endeavor would, of course, depend on the teaching staff and collaborative effort on the part of seminary administration "to ensure that this timely encounter with Scripture in the faith of the Church . . . can take place."[55]

Pope Benedict addresses the value of historical critical exegesis[56], a necessary access to the Bible, complemented by *lectio* in the same Spirit in which the Bible was written. The Bible is not Scripture simply in and of itself. It is the Word of God, when it is read in faith by the guidance of the Holy Spirit. On

54. Pope Benedict XVI, "Discourse of Pope Benedict XVI to the Bishops of Switzerland" (November 7, 2006), *L'Osservatore Romano* 29, no. 47 (November 22, 2006), pages 5 and 10, at 5.

55. Pope Benedict XVI, "Discourse of Pope Benedict XVI to the Bishops of Switzerland," 5 and 10.

56. Historical critical exegesis became a favorite in biblical research only beginning in the nineteenth century. "It became the dominant method for biblical studies taught to students in theological education only in the twentieth century. Therefore, Christians for most of the history of Christianity have not used the historical critical method in their readings of the Bible. To insist that historical criticism is necessary for the Christian reading of Scripture is to say that no Christian before the modern period read Scripture Christianly." Martin, *Pedagogy*, 43.

another occasion he states that what is needed is "a synthesis between an exegesis that operates with historical reason and an exegesis that is guided by faith. We have to bring the two things into a proper relationship to each other."[57] The goal of theological education for ministry, besides the formal study of the Bible, is to promote other, sometimes more theologically sensitive, ways of reading Scripture. To appreciate *lectio divina* we can learn from how believers in the early Church and throughout the Middle Ages thought about and interpreted Scripture, and this can "nurture and shape new imaginations for ourselves in scriptural interpretation."[58]

Dale Martin reflects on the challenge of reading Scripture today along the lines and with the same freedom as Christians have done throughout history. In answer to the question, What can contemporary readers and academic faculties learn from premodern approaches to Scripture? Martin responds, "Reading these interpreters helps us imagine how Christians can read Scripture without suffering from our normal anxiety about finding the right meaning of the text. These interpreters enter the space of Scripture looking for new inspiration, ways to think about God and their lives." Rather than fretting about the accuracy of the meaning of the text, according to the results of modern exegetical approaches, Martin suggests that Scripture is a space we can live in, something that directs our prayer, the Word of God speaking directly to the hearer or reader. And, ultimately "we could imagine Scripture as patient of many different meanings."[59]

The Word of God Addresses the Reader or Hearer in Community

Of the four stages in the traditional plan of *lectio divina* as outlined by Guigo the Carthusian—*lectio*, *meditatio*, *oratio*, and *contemplatio*—for the purposes of human formation, I pause with the *meditatio* stage. After reading Scripture, echoing the text by the repetition of words or phrases, enveloping the experience in recollection and silence, we may ask ourselves: Lord, what does this text have to do with my community and the Church? What troubles us about this text? How does this Scripture challenge our community to shift our consciousness in relation to the world and society? Why are we not interested in what this Word may be telling us? What do we as a community find pleasant and consoling in these words? How and why does this text move us?

57. Msgr. Charles Pope, "The Pope's View of the Historical-Critical Method of Biblical Interpretation" (December 17, 2010), at blog.adw.org/2010/12/the-popes-view-of-the-historical-critical-method-of-biblical-interpretation/.

58. Martin, *Pedagogy*, 45.

59. Martin, *Pedagogy*, 69–70.

Once we have set the Word of God in its ecclesial setting, one might turn to the personal hearing and reaction to the Word. What does this text have to do with me? How does this text address me now in my life? As is evident, I recommend a revision of the *lectio* in light of the tradition represented in Scripture, addressed to the Church in its communal nature. Examples of *lectio* in Scripture bear this out. Some prophetic books were composed along the style of *lectio*, as generation after generation read and reread the text in their actual situation. Thus, the book of Isaiah grew from a collection of oracles from the eighth century to oracles added over three or four centuries, to achieve the present form of the book. Centuries later, the Ethiopian eunuch read the Scriptures that were to him opaque, until Philip helped him with the interpretation, another example of collegial *lectio* (Acts 8:26–38).

Doubtless, the Scriptures have a lot to do with the individual in the search for truth and holiness, but to put it in proper sequence, the first question might be: What does this Word of God communicate to us, to the Church, today in our situation? What is God saying to our community now? In what ways does this text challenge us? In a second moment, we ask the classic question, "What does this text say to me?" How does it challenge me to conversion at this time in my life? The ecclesial concern in *lectio* is followed by that of the individual.

Ratio fundamentalis

The 2016 document *The Gift of the Priestly Vocation* (*Ratio fundamentalis*) addresses the value of priestly formation "in the spirit of the Gospel": For true pastoral care of the faithful, the priest needs to "internalize the spirit of the Gospel, thanks to a constant and personal friendship with Christ, leading him to share His sentiments and His attitudes." Thus, by contemplating Jesus, "who offered His life for others, he will be able to give himself generously and with self-sacrifice for God's people." How is the priest formed in the spirit of the Gospel? The Congregation for the Clergy answers, "The interior man needs to take special and faithful care of the interior spiritual life, centered principally on communion with Christ through the Mysteries celebrated in the course of the Liturgical Year, and nourished by personal prayer and meditation on the inspired Word." Silent prayer opens him to friendship with Christ and docility "to the action of the Spirit, which gradually molds him in the image of the Master."[60]

The formation process is traced as a path in interior transformation. "In

60. Congregation for the Clergy, *Ratio fundamentalis institutionis sacerdotalis* [The Gift of the Priestly Vocation] (December 8, 2016) (Vatican City: Libreria Editrice Vaticana), §41–42.

this way he will be able to choose, decide and act according to the will of God."[61] This journey calls for special attention to the care of the interior life by spiritual direction, personal prayer, and daily contact with the Word of God.

Even in the propaedeutic stage, familiarity with the Word of God should be considered "the soul and guide of the journey."[62] The Congregation emphasizes, "A relationship with the Word of God holds a preeminent place in the process of spiritual growth. Before it is ever preached, the Word must be welcomed in the depth of the heart." The new evangelization to which the Church is called today is the "point of reference for the life of discipleship and spiritual configuration to Christ the Good Shepherd." Those in formation come to know the Word through *lectio divina*. "A profound daily meditation, practised with fidelity and diligence, in which study and prayer come together in a reciprocal fruitfulness, will ensure an integral approach to both the Old and New Testaments."[63]

Lectio *Seminar Guided by the Lectionary*

The ample menu of the triennial Sunday lectionary offers a curricular panorama for imbuing the seminarian with the multifaceted world of Scripture. Between the two poles of the liturgical year, Lent-Easter and Advent-Christmas, stretch out the Sundays of Ordinary Time, during which the lectionary reads through the Bible in the course of three years. The gospel is the point of convergence of biblical revelation, and thus it is the reference for the choice of the first reading, which, except for the Easter season, is from the Old Testament.[64] In the triennial lectionary, the Old Testament in its major parts is represented and read through the lens of the gospel. In this way, Jesus' death and resurrection is the hermeneutical key to the Christian reading of the Old Testament. The risen Jesus gives the clue to reading the Old Testament in light of the Paschal mystery: the Emmaus episode of the two disciples on Easter morning (Luke 24:13–33; cf. vv. 32, 44–47).

Texts of the New Testament are selected as the second reading that, to an extent, echoes a salient theme of the first reading, the responsorial psalm, and the gospel. This organization around the gospel in the Sunday cycle consolidates the unity of the two Testaments.

In the interests of the seminary curriculum, I propose the *Lectio* Seminar

61. Congregation for the Clergy, *Ratio fundamentalis,* §43.

62. Congregation for the Clergy, *Ratio fundamentalis,* §59.

63. Congregation for the Clergy, *Ratio fundamentalis,* §103.

64. Selections from Acts of the Apostles make up the score of the first reading during the Easter season.

of the Old and the New Testaments, with texts selected from the current year of the Sunday lectionary. The seminar is designed to offer information and tools for a deeper appreciation of the biblical science and theology, with a view to the comprehension, interpretation, actualization, and personal appropriation of the Word of God. The objective of such a collegial exercise is to advance the reader's competence and familiarity with Scripture and equip a reader in his capacity for discernment, personal conversion, and ministry.

The content of the Seminar is the careful, prayerful study of the texts, situating them in their possible historical contexts, and relating them to companion texts in the lectionary, with the aim of illuminating the life and conversion of the participants. The Seminar focuses on reading and reflecting in a group. Mapped out by the triennial Sunday lectionary, it may last three years or six semesters.

The individual, preparing to be a minister of the Word, is encouraged to cultivate a friendship with the Word of God. "Knowledge of its linguistic or exegetical aspects, though certainly necessary, is not enough. He needs to approach the Word with a docile and prayerful heart so that it may deeply penetrate his thoughts and feelings and bring about a new outlook in him."[65]

Conclusion

In a parable, Jesus compares the word heard or read with the seed that is sown. He describes the different possibilities in the practice of *lectio*, the diverse ways of receiving the Word. In the interpretation Jesus emphasizes how the Word is received (Luke 8:12–15), the qualities of soil: the foot-trodden path; the hard, rocky ground; the patch of thorns; and the rich, fertile loam. Luke plows through the theological ground for the fertile word received in *lectio*, that was embraced with a generous and good heart, and bears fruit through perseverance.

In Scripture study there is a need for exploring the biblical text, using the methods at our disposal: linguistic, archeological, literary and rhetorical criticism, and canonical approaches. But finally, we read Scripture in the interests of ministry to a broken world, hungry for justice and well-being for all, thirsting for a Word of life. In our pedagogy of the Bible, along with critical, objective application of a method, the aim is that the hearer of the Word know himself and be drawn into the transformative process to which the Word of God invites him, so as to communicate to today's society and inspire the audience to enter a similar process of conversion and personal transformation.

65. Pope Francis, *Evangelii gaudium* [The Joy of the Gospel] (November 24, 2013) (New York: Image Books, 2014), §149.

Meditatio of *Lectio Divina* Following upon Exegesis-Informed *Lectio*: The Test Case of Romans 7:7–25

Marcin Kowalski

Does a prayerful reading of Scripture call for exegesis? What is the use of the latest exegetical tools and methodologies in discerning the invitation that God makes to man's heart through his Word? Is it not enough to read the biblical message with faith and an open heart, finding there a response to our present situation? The answer to these questions is important and has far-reaching consequences, both for our life of prayer and for our biblical studies. As the historical-critical school once dug an abyss between the Christ of faith and the Jesus of history, so today, we can inadvertently dig an abyss between the prayerful and the scientific reading of Scripture.

The two mentioned approaches should not be separated. The prayerful-only reading leads to rampant individualism; the scientific-only approach makes Scripture barren. Benedict XVI in *Verbum Domini* reminds us of the risk of individualism for someone who reads the Bible on his/her own. The first remedy indicated by the pope is "to read and experience sacred Scripture in communion with the Church."[1] The second remedy is the use of exegetical tools to discover the message encapsulated in the text itself. "Without this," contends the pope, "there is always a risk that the text will become a pretext for never moving beyond our own ideas."[2] The prayerful-only reading, which does not take into account the historicity and cultural background of the Bible, can easily turn into the fundamentalist interpretation criticized both in *Verbum Domini* and in the document issued by the Pontifical Biblical Commission, *The*

1. Pope Benedict XVI, *Verbum Domini* (September 30, 2010) (Washington, DC: United States Conference of Catholic Bishops, 2010), §86.

2. *Verbum Domini*, §87.

Interpretation of the Bible in the Church.[3] Thus Benedict, reminding us of the teaching of *Dei verbum*, encourages us to undertake a closer working relationship between pastors, exegetes, and theologians.[4]

The prayerful (personalizing) and the scientific (objectivizing) tendencies can be successfully bridged in the ancient tradition of *lectio divina*. This approach to Scripture presents us with an extremely valuable, time-tested model of how to read and teach the Bible today. *Lectio divina* fosters a critical reading of the Bible by putting *meditatio* in the context of community reading and placing it after *lectio*.[5] In the classical scheme presented to us again by the pope, *meditatio* deals with the question: what does the biblical text say to us? This question must be preceded by a thorough reading of the text (*lectio*), which illumines its content: what does the biblical text say in itself?[6] In *lectio divina* one does not think about doing *meditatio* (a prayerful reading of Scripture) independent of *lectio* (an informed or studied reading of Scripture). What biblical methodology reflects the synthesis between the scientific and prayerful approaches to Scripture present in *lectio divina*? What methodology could prove helpful to bridge the historical horizon of the text with that of the contemporary reader? To answer these questions let us have a look at the two particular approaches discussed by the Pontifical Biblical Commission: the historical-critical and the rhetorical readings of the Bible.

Historical-Critical and Rhetorical Readings of the Bible

The same preoccupations with the individualistic approach to the Bible expressed by Benedict XVI are also present in the previously mentioned document by the Pontifical Biblical Commission, *The Interpretation of the Bible in the Church*. This document deals with new approaches to the biblical text, divided into four categories:[7]

1) New methods of literary analysis (rhetorical, narrative, and semiotic analysis)
2) Approaches based on tradition (canonical approach, recourse to Jewish tradition of interpretation, and *Wirkungsgeschichte*)

3. *Verbum Domini*, §44.

4. *Verbum Domini*, §45.

5. For a description of the four classical stages of *lectio divina*, see *Verbum Domini*, §87.

6. See *Verbum Domini*, §87.

7. Pontifical Biblical Commission, *The Interpretation of the Bible in the Church* (Vatican City: Libreria Editrice Vaticana, 1993), §I.B–E.

3) Approaches that use human sciences (sociology, cultural anthropology, and psychological and psychoanalytical approaches)
4) Contextual approaches (liberationist and feminist approaches)

Besides these, the document mentions fundamentalist interpretation, which is severely criticized, and the historical-critical method, which, despite its shortcomings, is recommended as "indispensable" for making known the historical dynamism which animates sacred Scripture.[8] The document critiques this latter method for restricting itself "to a search for the meaning of the biblical text within the historical circumstances that gave rise to it" and neglecting other meanings and aspects of the text.[9] Yet, the Pontifical Biblical Commission still perceives the validity of this methodology in discovering the message expressed by the biblical authors and editors. Along with other methods and approaches, it is recommended as a tool to open up to the modern reader a path to the meaning of the biblical text.

The evaluation of the historical-critical method expressed in the document is very generous. The problem is that the historical-critical approach seems to be gradually disappearing from the scene of biblical studies. It is not without reason. Critiques of the method have been voiced for a long time by many scholars. Already in the 1950s, Amos Wilder made his now famous appeal for a more rhetorical and synchronic reading of the Bible in response to the fragmentation of the text caused by historical-critical studies.[10] The most severe critique of the method comes now from scholars operating in the field of postcolonial and socio-rhetorical studies. Accusations leveled against the historical-critical method include:

1) The method provided scholars with philological, grammatical, and historical tools with which everybody was supposed to reach the same objective conclusions, characteristic of the empirical disciplines. It led to the tyranny of historicism and to the confrontational elimination of other methods as non-scientific.
2) The historical-critical method eliminated the real reader and his/her cultural context as subjective and contaminating the objectivity of scientific analysis.

8. *The Interpretation of the Bible in the Church*, §I.A.

9. *The Interpretation of the Bible in the Church*, §I.A.4.

10. Cf. Vernon Kay Robbins, *The Tapestry of Early Christian Discourse: Rhetoric, Society, and Ideology* (London: Routledge, 1996), 2.

3) The historical-critical method proved to be incompatible with the nature and intention of the biblical text. It led to its deconstruction and had no tools to examine phenomena like miracles, revelation, and faith.

Some scholars contend that the historical-critical method has already become a footnote to the history of interpretation. Others claim that the method is dead in its axiological core, but its elements entered for good the workshop of every exegete. If not the historical-critical method, what other alternatives do we have to avoid sliding down into the all-individualistic reading of the Bible? One alternative can be found in the new rhetorical and socio-rhetorical approaches to the biblical text. If we were to describe schematically the methodological development that took place in the realm of biblical studies in the twentieth century, it could be compared to the Hegelian triad. From the historicity and diachronic reading embodied in the *Formgeschichte* (thesis), we passed to the more synchronic and individualistic reading (antithesis) (New Literary Criticism), to reach the synthesis, which is the combined textual and socio-historical approach (rhetoric and socio-rhetoric).[11] The exegetical workshop becomes more and more interdisciplinary, combining thorough textual analysis with the tradition-based, sociological, and anthropological approaches.

The Pontifical Biblical Commission's requirements to be attentive both to the variety of meanings and to the history present in the text, can be successfully met in the rhetorical and socio-rhetorical approaches.[12] What are the

11. Elizabeth S. Malbon and Edgar V. McKnight, eds., introduction to *The New Literary Criticism and the New Testament* (Valley Forge, PA: Trinity Press, 1994), 18.

12. On classical rhetoric and its use in biblical studies, see George A. Kennedy, *New Testament Interpretation through Rhetorical Criticism*, Studies in Religion (Chapel Hill: University of North Carolina Press, 1984); Burton L. Mack, *Rhetoric and the New Testament*, GBSNT (Minneapolis: Fortress Press, 1990); Stanley E. Porter and Thomas H. Olbricht, eds., *The Rhetorical Analysis of Scripture: Essays from the 1995 London Conference*, JSNTS 146 (Sheffield: Sheffield Academic, 1997); Stanley E. Porter, ed., *Handbook of Classical Rhetoric in the Hellenistic Period* (330 B. C.–A. D. 400) (Leiden: Brill, 1997); Stanley E. Porter and Thomas H. Olbricht, eds., *Rhetoric and the New Testament: Essays from the 1992 Heidelberg Conference*, JSNTS 90 (Sheffield: Sheffield Academic, 2001); Anders Eriksson, Thomas H. Olbricht, and Walter G. Übelacker, eds., *Rhetorical Argumentation in Biblical Texts: Essays from the Lund 2000 Conference*, ESEC 8 (Harrisburg, PA: Trinity Press, 2002); Thomas H. Olbricht and Anders Eriksson, eds., *Rhetoric, Ethic, and Moral Persuasion in Biblical Discourse: Essays from the 2002 Heidelberg Conference*, ESEC (New York: T&T Clark, 2005); Ben Witherington, *New Testament Rhetoric: An Introductory Guide to the Art of Persuasion in and of the New Testament* (Eugene: Cascade, 2009); J. Paul Sampley and Peter Lampe, *Paul and Rhetoric*, T&T Clark Biblical Studies (New York: T&T Clark, 2010); Troy W. Martin, ed., *Genealogies of New Testament Rhetorical Criticism* (Minneapolis: Fortress Press, 2014); Stanley E. Porter, ed., *Paul and Ancient Rhetoric:*

advantages of using rhetoric and socio-rhetoric in our analysis? Let us present them succinctly in five points:[13]

1) Rhetoric and socio-rhetoric take up the analytic tools of the historical-critical method (delimitation of a unit; structural analysis; *Sitz im Leben* and the genre of the text).
2) They are interested not in the archeology of the text, but in its present form. The text and the communicative strategies of the author are the primary field of inquiry. The basic advantage of rhetoric is that it does not treat the biblical text only as an artefact of written culture. It does justice both to the compositional character and to the nature of the text, in which, according to the latest research, the written and oral cultures overlap.[14] Classical rhetoric, used by the ancient authors, is also the most appropriate tool to read the meaning of such texts.
3) Rhetoric does not depart from history but looks for it in the analyzed text, not outside of it. The historical and socio-cultural data coming from the outside world can be applied to illumine the meaning of the text, but they remain a supplementary source of information. Rhetoric is cautious not to repeat the mistakes of the historical-critical method, where the center of gravity was oftentimes located far beyond the text itself. Such an approach resulted in anachronistic impositions of hypothetical, historical, and social models upon the analyzed text.

Theory and Practice in the Hellenistic Context (New York: Cambridge University Press, 2015). On the socio-rhetorical approach, see Robbins, *The Tapestry of Early Christian Discourse*; Vernon K. Robbins, *Exploring the Texture of Texts: A Guide to Socio-Rhetorical Interpretation* (Valley Forge, PA: Trinity Press, 1996).

13. Cf. Marcin Kowalski, *Transforming Boasting of Self into Boasting in the Lord: The Development of the Pauline Periautologia in 2 Cor 10–13*, SJ(L) (Lanham: University Press of America, 2013), 12–14.

14. On the rediscovery of orality in biblical studies, see e.g. R. C. Culley, "Oral Tradition and Biblical Studies," *Oral Tradition* 1, no. 1 (1986): 30–65; Casey Wayne Davis, *Oral Biblical Criticism: The Influence of the Principles of Orality on the Literary Structure of Paul's Epistle to the Philippians*, JSNTS 172 (Sheffield: Sheffield Academic, 1999), 11–63; Holly E. Hearon, "The Implications of 'Orality' for Studies of the Biblical Text," *Oral Tradition* 19, no. 1 (2004): 96–107; Terence C. Mournet, *Oral Tradition and Literary Dependency: Variability and Stability in the Synoptic Tradition and Q*, WUNT II/195 (Tübingen: Mohr Siebeck, 2005), 54–99; Kowalski, *Transforming Boasting of Self into Boasting in the Lord*, 14–21.

4) Rhetoric and socio-rhetoric are open to the reader's perspective, putting it in the context of the author's argumentative strategy. At its core, rhetoric is universal and ubiquitous in our present culture, thus bridging the horizons of the ancient and contemporary reader.

Since the authors of the New Testament lived and produced their writings in a "rhetorical culture,"[15] it is natural to turn to rhetoric as the most useful tool to interpret their texts. Thus, we do justice to *Dei verbum*'s appeal to read the biblical texts with the same intention and within the background in which they were created.[16] Let us turn then to discover the advantages of rhetoric when applied to a specific text. The test case will be the notoriously difficult Pauline passage Romans 7:7–25. How can a scientifically informed rhetorical exegesis help us in our meditation upon it? Focusing on Romans 7:7–25 we shall see how rhetoric guides us from falling into an "individualistic" reading of this complex passage.

Test Case: Romans 7:7–25

Romans 7:7–25 seems to come "out of the clear blue sky" in the midst of the Pauline description of the new life in Christ. After having argued that Christ is the only way of salvation for the entirety of mankind (Rom 1–4), in Rom 5–8 Paul shows the fruits of the justification brought by him.[17] Those who believe in Christ have peace with God and rejoice in the hope of sharing the divine glory (Rom 5:1–2). This hope cannot disappoint them because God's love has been poured into their hearts through the Holy Spirit (5:5). Justified by the blood of Christ, the believers will be saved from God's wrath (5:9). Further, Paul depicts Christians as baptized into Christ's death so as to be certainly united with him in a resurrection like his (6:4–5). In ch. 8, he even states that there is no condemnation for those who are in Christ Jesus (8:1) because the law of the Spirit liberated them from the law of sin and death (8:2). The believers are

15. The expression coined by Vernon K. Robbins, "Oral, Rhetorical, and Literary Cultures: A Response," *Semeia* 65 (1994): 75–91, at 80.

16. See Vatican II, *Dei verbum*, §12.

17. On the conceptual link between Rom 1–4 and 5–8, see James D. G. Dunn, *Romans 1–8*, WBC 38A (Dallas: Word, 1988), 89–95; Douglas J. Moo, *The Epistle to the Romans*, NICNT (Grand Rapids: Eerdmans, 1996), 290–292; C. E. B. Cranfield, *A Critical and Exegetical Commentary on the Epistle to the Romans: Introduction and Commentary on Romans I–VIII*, ICC (Edinburgh: T&T Clark, 2004), 252–254; Jean-Noël Aletti, *God's Justice in Romans: Keys for Interpreting the Epistle to the Romans*, SubBi 37 (Rome: Gregorian & Biblical Press, 2010), 44–56.

called the sons of God and fellow heirs with Christ, destined to share in his glory (8:14–17). The treatise on the new life in Christ finishes with a magnificent hymn praising God's love, from which the believers cannot be separated by any earthly or heavenly power (8:31–39).

In the midst of this impressive image, however, the cry of desperation breaks out. The human "ego" intones quite a different song in which it depicts itself as fraught with all kinds of covetousness (7:8), deceived and struck with death by sin which manipulated the Law (7:9–13). The tragic character portrayed in Rom 7 is carnal and one sold under sin (7:14). He (or she) does not understand his own actions (7:15); he can will what is right but he cannot do it (7:18). Being paralyzed by sin, he commits the evil he does not want to do (7:19–20). There is a war that he perceives in his members making him captive to the law of sin which dwells within him (7:23). At the end, the paralyzed and mortified individual emits a heartbreaking cry: "Wretched man that I am! Who will deliver me from this body of death?" (7:24 RSV).

What is the identity of the "ego" which speaks in such dramatic tones? Many exegetes in numberless publications have sought to give an answer to this question.[18] Their efforts can be generally subsumed under four categories:[19]

18. On the rhetorical "I" in Rom 7, see Werner Georg Kümmel, *Römer 7 und Das Bild des Menschen im Neuen Testament: Zwei Studien*, TB 53 (München: C. Kaiser, 1974); Jules M. Cambier, "Le 'Moi' dans Rom. 7," 13–72 in *The Law of the Spirit in Rom 7 and 8*, ed. Jules-Marie Cambier and Bucks Langley (Rome: St. Paul's Abbey, 1976); D. H. Campbell, "The Identity of 'egō' in Romans 7,7–25," 57–64 in *Studia Biblica* 1978: *Sixth International Congress on Biblical Studies*, vol. 3, *Paper on Paul and Other New Testament Authors*, ed. E. A. Livingston, JSNTS 3 (Sheffield: Sheffield Academic, 1980); Mark A. Seifrid, "The subject of Rom 7:14–25," *Novum Testamentum* 34, no. 4 (1992): 313–333; Don B. Garlington, *Faith, Obedience, and Perseverance: Aspects of Paul's Letter to the Romans*, WUNT II/79 (Tübingen: Mohr Siebeck, 1994), 111–112; Michael Paul Middendorf, *The "I" in the Storm: A Study of Romans* 7 (St. Louis: Concordia, 1997); Jean-Noël Aletti, "Romans 7:7–25 and Galatians 5:17: Questions and Proposals," 79–109 in *New Approaches for Interpreting the Letters of Saint Paul: Collected Essays Rhetoric, Soteriology, Christology and Ecclesiology*, SubBi 43 (Rome: Gregorian & Biblical Press, 2012); Michael Winger, "Paul and ἐγώ: Some Comments on Grammar and Style," *New Testament Studies* 63, no. 1 (2017): 23–37.

19. Cf. Joseph A. Fitzmyer, *Romans: A New Translation with Introduction and Commentary*, AncB 33 (New York: Doubleday, 1993), 463–466; Moo, *The Epistle to the Romans*, 424–431; Thomas R. Schreiner, *Romans*, BECNT 6 (Grand Rapids: Baker Books, 1998), 359–365, 379–392; Cranfield, *A Critical and Exegetical Commentary on the Epistle to the Romans*, 342–347; Ben Witherington and Darlene Hyatt, *Paul's Letter to the Romans: A Socio-Rhetorical Commentary* (Grand Rapids: Eerdmans, 2004), 179–196; Robert Jewett and Roy David Kotansky, *Romans: A Commentary on the Book of Romans, Hermeneia* (Minneapolis: Fortress Press, 2007), 441–445.

1) The autobiographical "ego": Paul describes his own experience, his pharisaic past and the requirements of the Law which overwhelmed him and brought him to conversion at Damascus[20]
2) The "ego" denoting Israel: Paul describes the experience of Israel after the gift of the Law at Sinai[21]
3) The Adamic "ego": Paul describes the experience of mankind confronted with the requirements of the Law[22]

20. Cf. Robert H. Gundry, "The Moral Frustration of Paul before His Conversion: Sexual Lust in Romans 7:7–25," 228–245 in *Pauline Studies: Essays Presented to Professor F.F. Bruce on His 70th Birthday*, ed. F. F. Bruce, Donald A. Hagner, and Murray J. Harris (Exeter/Grand Rapids: Paternoster/Eerdmans, 1980), 229; Dunn, *Romans 1–8*, 382–383; Alan F. Segal, *Paul the Convert: The Apostolate and Apostasy of Saul the Pharisee* (New Haven: Yale University Press, 1990), 225; C. K. Barrett, *The Epistle to the Romans*, 2nd ed., rev. ed., BNTC 6 (London: Hendrickson Publisher, 1991), 134–135; Jan Lambrecht, *The Wretched "I" and Its Liberation: Paul in Romans* 7 and 8, LThPM 14 (Louvain: Peeters, 1992), 90; Moo, *The Epistle to the Romans*, 431, 447–448; Jean-Noël Aletti, "Romans 7, 7–25: Rhetorical Criticism and Its Usefulness," *Svensk exegetisk årsbok* 61 (1996): 77–95, at 90–91; Schreiner, *Romans*, 365; Cranfield, *A Critical and Exegetical Commentary on the Epistle to the Romans*, 345; Jewett and Kotansky, *Romans*, 440–445.

21. Cf. Jan Lambrecht, "Man before and without Christ: Romans 7 and Pauline Anthropology," *Louvain Studies* 5 (1974): 18–33; Mark W. Karlberg, "Israel's History Personified: Romans 7:7–13 in Relation to Paul's Teaching on the 'Old Man'," *Trinity Journal* 7, no. 1 (1986): 65–74, at 68–69; Barrett, *The Epistle to the Romans*, 134–135; Walt Russell, "Insights from Postmodernism's Emphasis on Interpretive Communities in the Interpretation of Romans 7," *Journal of the Evangelical Theological Society* 37, no. 4 (1994): 511–527, at 523; Brendan Byrne, *Romans*, SaPaSe 6 (Collegeville, MN: Liturgical Press, 1996), 218; Moo, *The Epistle to the Romans*, 431, 447–448 (Paul's solidarity with Israel).

22. Cf. Stanislas Lyonnet, "L'histoire du salut selon le chapitre 7 de l'épître aux Romains," *Biblica* 43, no. 2 (1962): 117–151; Rudolf Schnackenburg, "Römer 7 in Zusammenhang des Römerbriefes," in *Jesus und Paulus: Festschrift fur Werner Georg Kummel zum 70. Geburstag*, ed. E. E. Ellis and Erich Grässer (Gottingen: Vandenhoeck & Ruprecht, 1975), 293–294; Paul J. Achtemeier, *Romans*, Int. (Atlanta: John Knox Press, 1985), 122; John A. Ziesler, "The Role of the Tenth Commandment in Romans 7," *Journal for the Study of the New Testament* 33 (1988): 41–56, at 45; Dunn, *Romans 1–8*, 378–384; Don B. Garlington, "Romans 7:14–25 and the Creation Theology of Paul," *Trinity Journal* 11, no. 2 (1990): 197–235, at 207–210; Bruce W. Longenecker, *Eschatology and the Covenant: A Comparison of 4 Ezra and Romans 1–11*, JSNTS 57 (Sheffield: Sheffield Academic, 1991), 237–239; Barrett, *The Epistle to the Romans*, 134–135; Seifrid, "The subject of Rom 7:14–25," 149; Timo Laato, *Paul and Judaism: An Anthropological Approach*, SFSHJ 115 (Atlanta: Scholars Press, 1995), 170–175; Christian Grappe, "Qui me délivrera de ce corps de mort? L'esprit de vie! Romains 7,24 et 8,2 comme éléments de typologie adamique," *Biblica* 83, no. 4 (2002): 472–492; Witherington and Hyatt, *Paul's Letter to the Romans*, 179, 187–190; Hermann Lichtenberger, *Das Ich Adams und das Ich der Menschheit: Studien zum Menschenbild in Römer 7*, WUNT II/164 (Tübingen: Mohr Siebeck, 2004), 107–186.

4) The Christian "ego": Paul describes the experience of Christians facing the requirements of the new life in Christ (Augustine, Thomas Aquinas, Luther, Calvin, Melanchthon)[23]

Let us have a general look at each of the major interpretative options with special attention paid to the last one. Is it possible that the "ego" speaking in Rom 7 is actually Paul's own voice, the testimony of his pharisaic experience? The autobiographical hypothesis has been significantly weakened by Werner Kümmel, who referred to passages like Gal 1:13–14 or Phil 3:4–6 where Paul boasts of his pharisaic roots.[24] Another severe blow came from Kirster Stendahl, who coined the famous phrase "the introspective conscience of the West," and said it was imposed on Paul in the inquiries regarding his past.[25] Despite the former criticism, Robert Jewett and Douglas Moo claim that the autobiographical hypothesis is coming into vogue again through a more elaborate version.[26] Troels Engberg-Pedersen even states that contemporary research has proved beyond any reasonable doubt that in Rom 7:7–25 Paul speaks from his Christian point of view and describes his pharisaic past.[27] Jewett perceives here Paul the zealot, whose zeal for the Law brought him to stand against the Messiah.[28]

It is surely not Paul, a frustrated Pharisee, who speaks in Rom 7:7–25, but

23. Cf. David Wenham, "The Christian Life: A Life of Tension? A Consideration of the Nature of Christian Experience in Paul," in Bruce, Hagner, and Harris, *Pauline Studies*, 80–94; David S. Dockery, "Romans 7:14–25: Pauline Tension in the Christian Life," *Grace Theological Journal* 2, no. 2 (1981): 239–257; John M. Espy, "Paul's 'Robust Conscience' Re-Rxamined," *New Testament Studies* 31, no. 2 (1985): 171–175; Dunn, *Romans 1–8*, 387–399, 403– 412; Garlington, *Faith, Obedience, and Perseverance*, 110–143; Barrett, *The Epistle to the Romans*, 137–144; Robert H. Mounce, *Romans*, NAC 27 (Nashville,: Broadman & Holman, 1995), 167–168; Schreiner, *Romans*, 390; Laato, *Paul and Judaism*, 109–145; Lauri Thurén, *Derhetorizing Paul: A Dynamic Perspective on Pauline Theology and the Law*, WUNT II/124 (Tübingen: Mohr Siebeck, 2000), 117–126; Cranfield, *A Critical and Exegetical Commentary on the Epistle to the Romans*, 341–347, 355–370; John F. Hart, "Paul as Weak in Faith in Romans 7:7–25," *Bibliotheca Sacra* 170, no. 679 (2013): 317–343.

24. See Kümmel, *Römer 7 und Das Bild des Menschen im Neuen Testament*. See the critique of Kümmel in Espy, "Paul's 'Robust Conscience' Re-Examined," 161–188; Aletti, "Romans 7,7–25: Rhetorical Criticism and Its Usefulness," 89.

25. Cf. Stendahl, "The Apostle Paul and the Introspective Conscience of the West," *Harvard Theological Review* 56 (1963): 199–215.

26. Cf. Moo, *The Epistle to the Romans*, 444; Jewett and Kotansky, *Romans*, 444–445.

27. See Troels Engberg-Pedersen, "The Reception of Graeco-Roman Culture in the New Testament: The Case of Romans 7.7–25," 32–57 in *The New Testament as Reception*, ed. Mogens Müller and Henrik Tronier, JSNTS 230 (London: Sheffield Academic, 2002), 37.

28. See Jewett and Kotansky, *Romans*, 444–445.

it might be Paul who now perceives his past without Christ as futile and leading to ultimate doom. If we read Rom 7 in unity with Rom 1–4, which defeats the Jewish way of salvation through Law, we see that Paul has also found himself in the group condemned by the Law. The cry of "ego" in Rom 7:7–25 is a cry of solidarity with Israel, which brings us to the second interpretation: "ego" denoting Jews who cannot save themselves by practicing the deeds of the Law. They are alluded to especially in the first part of the Pauline argumentation where the notion of Law frequently appears (7:1–13).[29] The drama of Law and commandment which proved helpless in the face of sin captures well the experience of Israel and the broken covenants of its past.

At the same time, however, the vocabulary used by Paul opens his argumentation to yet another, third interpretative option of "ego."[30] Right at the beginning, in Rom 7:1 *nomos* appears without an article, which can mean both Roman and Jewish law. The pagans can easily find themselves in the experience of living under religious or philosophical laws, which pose requirements without giving strength to fulfill them. Further, in the second part of Paul's argumentation, Rom 7:13–25, the language of *nomos* is supplemented with the universal language of good and evil (7:16, 18, 19, 21).[31] It speaks not only to the Jews, but also to Greeks and Romans, and practitioners of Hellenistic cults and philosophies, who experience the radical incapacity to do good. Being carnal and sold to the slavery of her instincts, the person does not understand herself and does not do what she wills (7:14–15). Commentators spot here an allusion to Medea's complaint from Ovid's *Metamorphoses* 7.19–21: "Oh, if I could, I would be more like myself! But against my own wishes, some strange influence weighs heavily upon me, and desire sways one way, reason another. . . . I see the better and approve; the worse I follow."[32] The wretched "I" comprises both Jewish and pagan experience. Can we hear in its cry the Christian voice too?

29. Cf. Dunn, *Romans 1–8*, 359; Barrett, *The Epistle to the Romans*, 126; Moo, *The Epistle to the Romans*, 410; Schreiner, *Romans*, 346; Cranfield, *A Critical and Exegetical Commentary on the Epistle to the Romans*, 333.

30. Cf. Fitzmyer, *Romans*, 455–456; Jean-Noël Aletti, "The Rhetoric of Romans 5–8," 294–308 in Porter and Olbricht, *The Rhetorical Analysis of Scripture*, esp. 300; Aletti, "Romans 7:7–25 and Galatians 5:17," 79–109 in *New Approaches for Interpreting the Letters of Saint Paul*, 89–105. See also Lambrecht, "Man before and without Christ: Romans 7 and Pauline Anthropology," 18–33.

31. Cf. Fitzmyer, *Romans*, 463; Witherington and Hyatt, *Paul's Letter to the Romans*, 199–205.

32. Cited in Witherington and Hyatt, *Paul's Letter to the Romans*, 205. See also Charles H. Talbert, *Romans*, Smyth & Helwys Bible Commentary (Macon, GA: Smyth & Helwys, 2002), 193; Jewett and Kotansky, *Romans*, 468.

Such a question brings us to the fourth interpretation of the Christian "ego." This interpretation is particularly important given our broader purposes, since an initial prayerful reading of the passage by a believer will naturally tend in this direction. According to commentators this fourth interpretation is supported by the following argumentation:[33]

1) The present tense used by Paul in vv. 14–25 cannot be anything else but the description of the present condition of the Christian addressees.
2) The thanksgiving for Christ in v. 7:25a and the following phrase v. 7:25b, "I of myself serve the law of God with my mind, but with my flesh I serve the law of sin," cannot come from any other than a Christian subject.
3) "Delight in the law of God" in v. 7:22 can refer only to a Jew or Christian, not to a pagan.
4) Rom 7:14–25 describes the Christian life of grace which still awaits its full revelation, as indicated by v. 7:24: "Who will deliver me from this body of death?"
5) We should read Rom 7 in the context of Rom 5–8, whose main topic is the new life in Christ.
6) Rom 7:14–25 can be compared to Galatians 5:16–18, which also portrays Christians living according to the flesh and according to the Spirit.
7) The last argument is an existential one: many Christians can identify with the images of internal struggle in Rom 7.

Given the above-mentioned arguments, when praying with Rom 7:7–25 one naturally tends to read this chapter as his/her own experience. If the great apostle Paul describes himself as torn and imprisoned by sin, how much more so does this apply to us?

At this point, rhetorically-oriented exegesis offers various instruments that invalidate the existential Christian interpretation of Rom 7:7–25. First, the present tense used by Paul does not necessarily indicate the condition of the audience. It can also be a rhetorical tool to engage the listeners as participants in the vividly described drama. Second, given the broad concept of *nomos* used by the apostle, "the delight" in the divine laws can also characterize pagans. Third, the link between Rom 7:14–25 and Gal 5:16–18 is problematic because the latter passage does not portray Christians as living under the power of sin. Fourth, the strongest argument for the Christian "ego" is Rom 7:25. However,

33. Cf. Moo, *The Epistle to the Romans*, 446; Schreiner, *Romans*, 379–384.

the thanksgiving for Christ in Rom 7:25a can be defined as a rhetorical anticipation of Rom 8, and followed by Rom 7:26b where Paul returns to the description of the "wretched" Jewish or pagan individual.[34]

What ultimately remains is the argument saying that Rom 7 should be read in the context of Rom 5–8, which describes the new life in Christ and thus refers to the Christian experience. It is here where rhetoric can be of great use to illumine the meaning of the chapter at issue. What is being exposed in Rom 7:7–25 has actually been foreshadowed and announced by Paul in Rom 5. This programmatic chapter plays the role of introduction to the entire discourse in Rom 5–8. In Rom 5:1–11, which can be qualified as an *exordium*, the apostle depicts the fruits of justification.[35] The believers rejoice in being at peace with God, having access to his grace and certainty of future glory and salvation. The *exordium* plays two principal roles: first, it introduces the topics that will be elaborated by Paul in the course of his argumentation (justification, hope, Spirit, death, sin, life); second, it assures the speaker of the warm welcome of the audience. Paul speaks in the first person plural ("we"), identifying himself with the believers who share in common the experience of the abundance of God's grace.

This ideal image of Christian life, which dominates the *exordium* and stresses the greatness of God's gift, is then followed by the description of the human world in which two figures are contrasted: Adam and Christ. We can then pass on to the next part of Paul's speech (5:12–19), which can be labeled as a rhetorical *narratio*.[36] The rhetorical function of a *narratio* is that the orator presents what happened, what probably took place, or the circumstances concerning the debated issue.[37] The *narratio* can bear polemic tones and it prepares for the main thesis of the speech (which in our case is 5:20–21).[38] A *narratio* is

34. Cf. Moo, *The Epistle to the Romans*, 466–467; Witherington and Hyatt, *Paul's Letter to the Romans*, 196.

35. Cf. Aletti, *God's Justice in Romans*, 52; Andrzej Gieniusz, *Romans 8:18–30: "Suffering Does Not Thwart the Future Glory,"* University of South Florida International Studies in Formative Christianity and Judaism 9 (Atlanta: Scholars Press, 1999), 35–39; Jewett and Kotansky, *Romans*, 344 (Introduction).

36. Cf. Aletti, "The Rhetoric of Romans 5–8," 302–304; Gieniusz, *Romans 8:18–30*, 34–35.

37. Cf. Aletti, *God's Justice in Romans*, 52. On *narratio* in classical rhetoric, see Aristotle, *Rhetorica* 3.13.3–5; 16.1–11; Cicero, *Rhetorica ad Herennium* 1.8.12–9.16; Cicero, *De Inventione Rhetoricā* 1.19.27–22.31; Quintilian, *Institutiones Oratoriae* 4.2; Heinrich Lausberg, David E. Orton, and R. Dean Anderson, *Handbook of Literary Rhetoric: A Foundation for Literary Study* (Leiden: Brill, 1998), §289.

38. Cf. Aletti, "The Rhetoric of Romans 5–8," 300–302; Aletti, *God's Justice in Romans*, 51–52; Gieniusz, *Romans 8:18–30*, 39, 41. On *propositio* in ancient speech, see Aristotle, *Rhet.* 1.3.7; Quintilian, *Inst.* 4.4.1–9; Lausberg, Orton and Anderson, *Handbook of Literary Rhetoric*, §346.

precisely the role of Rom 5:12–19, where the situation of the human world is presented in much more dramatic tones than in the preceding *exordium*. Paul, by using the technique of *synkrisis,* puts against each other Adam and Christ. The former is responsible for spreading the dominion of sin and death (5:12–14); the latter brings the superabundance of grace which grants life-giving justification (5:15–19).

Even though Adam seems to be only a background for Christ, in the *narratio* Paul depicts mankind under two powers: the fatal power of sin and the salvific power of God. Now, the comparison drawn in ch. 5 will continue, constituting a conceptual frame in which the whole discourse of Rom 5–8 should be read. It has been aptly shown as such by Jean-Noël Aletti, who proposed the following scheme to trace the train of Paul's thought in these chapters:[39]

Rom 5:1–11:	*Exordium*: The new life in Christ
Rom 5:12–19:	*Narratio*: Adam vs. Christ
Rom 5:20–21:	*Thesis:* The reign of grace over the reign of sin and Law
Rom 6–8:	*Argumentatio*: The sinful man vs. free humanity
Rom 6:1–7:6:	Proof 1: *The new humanity* in Christ, free from sin
Rom 7:7–25:	Proof 2: *The old man* delivered up to sin, still subject to the Law
Rom 8:1–30:	Proof 3: *The new humanity* integrated into the family of God
Rom 8:31–39:	*Peroratio*: The final victory of the new life in Christ

What is striking here is the rhetorical technique of *synkrisis* (comparison) that dominates Paul's entire discourse in Rom 5–8. Rom 5:15–21 describes the reign of grace in the life of those who are in Christ and at the same time prepares the proofs of Rom 6:1–7:6 and Rom 8. In Rom 6, Paul accentuates the new identity of the baptized who, being in Christ, cannot subject themselves to the rule of sin and death. In Rom 8, the apostle introduces the Holy Spirit as the one who enables Christians to walk in the newness of life. On the opposite side, Rom 5:12–14 describes the dramatic situation of those outside of Christ, which will be explicated in Rom 7:7–25. The protagonists of Rom 6:1–7:6 and Rom 8 are the baptized, whose life is marked by reference to Christ's grace and Spirit. The "ego" speaking in Rom 7:7–25 is imprisoned by sin and deprived of Christ. It relates to Adam and comprises the cry of the entirety of humanity without the Savior. The *synkrisis* between the old and new humanity is the conceptual tool with which we should read Rom 5–8. It is also foreshadowed in Rom

39. Aletti, "The Rhetoric of Romans 5–8," 304. See also Witherington and Hyatt, *Paul's Letter to the Romans*, 207–208.

7:5–6, which comprises the *partitio*, whose rhetorical function is to give a brief announcement of the topics to follow, which in this case are those treated in Rom 7:7–8:30:[40]

a = v. 5 (in the past) life in the flesh, sinful passions, Law, and death
b = v. 6 (now) discharged from the Law, in the new life of the Spirit
A = 7:1–25 death, sin, passions, and Law
B = 8:1–30 Spirit and life

This way, Rom 7:7–25 is not an unexpected incision or digression in Paul's exposition of the new life in Christ, but an element of the powerful comparison between the two kinds of humanity introduced already in Rom 5:12–21. On the one side, we see humanity characterized by the indwelling of sin, incapable of practicing the Law, living according to the flesh, subject to death and the slavery of sin. On the other side, by using the same language, Paul depicts the new humanity characterized by the indwelling of the Spirit, capable of accomplishing the Law, living according to the Spirit, endowed with life, sonship, and inheritance.[41]

Taking into consideration the argumentative strategy of Paul, one can discard the interpretation that hears the cries of the Christian "ego" in Rom 7:7–25.[42] The Christian experience differs in every aspect from the one described there. Even if Christians still struggle for the sanctity of their lives, they are not so dramatically torn, humiliated, and enslaved to sin as the "ego" described in Rom 7:7–25. There is no *simul iustus et peccator* in Christians, because they are sanctified by Christ and they call themselves sons of God. The tension they still face refers to the humbleness and imperfection of the present state as compared to the glory and completion it will reach in heaven. It is the tension of the new life which will be resolved only at the end of time. Thanks to the comparison, the believers can fully appreciate the liberating power of God and freedom

40. Aletti, "The Rhetoric of Romans 5–8," 300; Gieniusz, *Romans 8:18–30*, 43.

41. Cf. Jean-Noël Aletti, "Romans 8: The Incarnation and Its Redemptive Impact," 111–138 in *New Approaches for Interpreting the Letters of Saint Paul: Collected Essays Rhetoric, Soteriology, Christology and Ecclesiology*, SubBi 43 (Rome: Gregorian & Biblical Press, 2012), 113.

42. On the non-Christian rhetorical "ego" in Rom 7:7–25, see also B. W. Longenecker, *Rhetoric at the Boundaries: The Art and Theology of New Testament Chain-Link Transitions* (Waco: Baylor University Press, 2005), 92–93; Justin King, "Rhetorical Chain-Link Construction and the Relationship between Romans 7.1–6 and 7.7–8.39: Additional Evidence for Assessing the Argument of Romans 7–8 and the Identity of the Infamous 'I'," *Journal for the Study of the New Testament* 39, no. 3 (2017): 258–278, at 275.

they have when living in Christ. Without him, theirs would be the dramatic cry of the "ego" described in Rom 7:24: "Wretched man that I am! Who will deliver me from this body of death?"

Conclusions

To conclude, the test case of Rom 7:7–25 is instrumental for understanding two things. The first is the insufficiency of *meditatio* (prayerful-only reading) without *lectio* (exegetical reading). Taking Rom 7:7–25 at face value, one naturally reads it as a present Christian experience additionally validated by our personal struggles with sin. Many Christians identify with the cry of the "ego" on an existential and experiential basis. That is why we may call such an interpretation "individualistic": because it does not move beyond one's own limited personal horizon. In fact, Paul wants us to move beyond it, and he challenges our views on Christian life. It has nothing to do with the broken existence and torn identity of those who live outside Christ. In order to spot the main point of Paul's argument we need to start from *lectio*, a thorough exegetical analysis.

Secondly, as we saw, classic exegesis is not enough in the case of Paul, who thinks and writes in terms of rhetorical culture. Paul's thought must be studied with the same tools that he used to shape it. Thus, we stress the usefulness of the rhetorical method. Rhetoric by nature is the art of the word and serves nothing less than to introduce us to the heart of God's word. When in our *lectio divina* we read Rom 7:7–25 through the lens of rhetoric, our *meditatio* turns into appreciation of God's gifts and thanksgiving.

Illumined by such conclusions, our prayerful reading of Rom 7:7–25 opens itself to the following considerations:

1) In Rom 7 Paul depicts the human "ego" as deceived and killed by sin (Rom 7:7–13), torn between delight in the law of God and the incapacity to follow it (Rom 7:21–23). What is my approach to the laws and commandments of the Lord? Do I not fall into the pit of Jewish or pagan self-justification by relying on my human strength when trying to live according to the Gospel? The Holy Spirit is the one who liberates Christians from the incapacity to obey the commandments (Rom 8:2–4) and the futile human struggle to sanctify their own lives. Walking according to the Spirit (Rom 8:4–8), discovering his power, and embracing it make the difference between Christian conduct and that of any other sort.

2) In Rom 7 Paul describes the individual as sold into slavery under sin (Rom 7:14) which dwells within him/her (Rom 7:17) and paralyzes his/her will (Rom 7:17–20). How do I live and cope with the reality of sin in my life? Sin can threaten our Christian existence but we are not enslaved to it anymore. By baptism, we were baptized into Christ's death and resurrection to walk in newness of life (Rom 6:3–4). The one who dies with Christ is freed from sin (Rom 6:7). Christians consider themselves as dead to sin and alive to God in Christ (Rom 6:11). They live under grace, not under sin (Rom 6:15), and they are slaves of God and his righteousness (Rom 6:18, 22). Thanks to the gift of the Holy Spirit, they actually belong to Christ; Christ and the Spirit, not sin, dwell within them (Rom 8:9). The same Spirit bears witness that they are the sons of God (Rom 8:14–17).
3) Finally, in Rom 7 Paul portrays the struggle that takes place in the person who does not understand his or her own actions and does what he or she hates (Rom 7:15), wretched and imprisoned in the body of death (Rom 7:24). How do I live through my internal struggles and crises? Christian struggles differ from pagan ones in terms of both purpose and the way of living through them. Christians still experience the weakness and suffering of this world, but they see them in the perspective of the Kingdom of God. The Spirit accompanies their struggles with the assurance that they work for the revelation of the glory of God (Rom 8:18). The groaning of creation, in which believers also participate, is being transformed into a prayer thanks to the Spirit (Rom 8:23). When Christians do not know how to pray, the Spirit intercedes for them before God with sighs too deep for words (Rom 8:25). The struggle ceases to be a desperate battle with one's weakness and turns into the acceptance of our humble present condition and the patient expectation of the fullness of life in heaven.

Thanksgiving, instead of lamentation, is the difference between a well-prepared *meditatio* on Rom 7:7–25 and a *meditatio* based only on our own intuition. In the prayerful reading of Rom 7 we are called to praise God for the undeserved and super-generous gift of new life in Christ which liberates us from the tyranny of Law and sin. Those in Christ should never forget what riches of grace have been opened to them. For that reason Paul compares the new life in Christ to the life of the old man sold to sin. It serves as a dark background to highlight the brightness and novelty of our present Christian existence.

Oratio and *Contemplatio* (and *Actio*) of *Lectio Divina*

Daniel Keating

Introduction

The topic I was asked to address is: *oratio* and *contemplatio* (and *actio*) of *lectio divina* following upon exegesis-informed *lectio*. It is important to begin with the words of *Verbum Domini*, both because they are extremely rich in their own right and because they provide the essential orientation to our topic. In paragraph 82, Pope Benedict proposes a fundamental orientation to the study and reception of Scripture:

> "Candidates for the priesthood must learn to love the word of God. Scripture should thus be the soul of their theological formation, and emphasis must be given to the indispensable interplay of exegesis, theology, spirituality and mission." Those aspiring to the ministerial priesthood are called to a profound personal relationship with God's word, particularly in *lectio divina*, so that this relationship will in turn nurture their vocation.[1]

The language here of loving the word of God and having a personal relationship with it demands more than intellectual understanding alone; it shows an embrace of God's word with all of one's heart, soul, mind, and strength.

1. Pope Benedict XVI, *Verbum Domini* (September 30, 2010) (Washington, DC: United States Conference of Catholic Bishops, 2010), §82. The opening quotation from this selection comes from the *Final Propositions of the Synod of Bishops on the Bible* (no. 32). Benedict, thus, takes the concern of the bishops for loving the word of God and expands on this by showing the role of *lectio divina* in gaining this love. For the English translation of the *Propositions*, see John L. Allen, Jr., "Final Propositions of the Synod of Bishops on the Bible," *National Catholic Reporter* (October 27, 2008), at www.ncronline.org/news/synod-final-propositions-synod-bishops-bible.

Benedict then proceeds to underline the crucial interrelationship between study and prayer:

> The Synod recommended that seminarians be concretely helped to see *the relationship between biblical studies and scriptural prayer*. The study of Scripture ought to lead to an increased awareness of the mystery of divine revelation and foster an attitude of prayerful response to the Lord who speaks. . . . Hence, great care should be taken to ensure that seminarians always cultivate this *reciprocity between study and prayer* in their lives.[2]

Embedded here is the topic I was asked to pursue: How do the reading and study of Scripture work together with prayer for a full reception of the word of God and for preparation for active mission? Benedict adds another crucial element to this picture by drawing our attention to the need for a *communal* reading of Scripture, and therefore, for responsive prayer that is always corporately aware: "While it is a word addressed to each of us personally, it is also a word which builds community, which builds the Church. Consequently, *the sacred text must always be approached in the communion of the Church*."[3]

Then we come to the specific text where Benedict coordinates the Latin terms in an ordered, ascending pattern. He offers a process beginning with *lectio*, moving to *meditatio*, then advancing to *oratio* and *contemplatio*, but without neglecting the outcome expressed in *actio*.[4] I will return to the descriptions Benedict supplies for these discrete stages, but first I wish to pursue briefly the question that immediately arose in my mind when I read Benedict's words: What is the source of these terms and their ordering in this particular way? Is this a construction of Benedict's making or does it arise from the tradition, and if the latter, from where in the tradition?

Guigo II, *The Ladder of Monks*, and the Four Stages

Searching through various sources, I discovered that a Carthusian monk of the twelfth century, Guigo II, penned a work that outlines the spiritual life of the monk according to just these four Latin terms: *lectio*, *meditatio*, *oratio*, and *contemplatio*. Guigo was prior of the Grande Chartreuse from 1174–1180. The work he authored is titled *The Ladder of Monks* (*Scala Claustralium*), also known by the title *The Ladder of Paradise*. At points variously attributed to Augustine, Bernard of Clairvaux, and Anselm, *The Ladder of Monks* was widely read in the

2. *Verbum Domini*, §82, emphasis in the original.
3. *Verbum Domini*, §86, emphasis in the original.
4. *Verbum Domini*, §87.

Middle Ages and became a favorite of the *devotio moderna* movement and the Brethren of the Common Life.[5]

In this short work, replete with scriptural citation, Guigo begins by stating that he is offering his "thoughts on the spiritual exercises proper to cloistered monks."[6] Attributing the schema of four stages to a revelation that came to him all at once, he lays out the stages concisely:

> Reading [*lectio*] is the careful study of the Scriptures, concentrating all one's powers on it. Meditation [*meditatio*] is the busy application of the mind to seek with the help of one's own reason for knowledge of hidden truth. Prayer [*oratio*] is the heart's devoted turning to God to drive away evil and obtain what is good. Contemplation [*contemplatio*] is when the mind is in some sort lifted up to God and held above itself, so that it tastes the joys of everlasting sweetness.[7]

Not content with this analytical description, Guigo proceeds to describe the four rungs of the ladder in terms of the metaphor of tasting:

> Reading seeks for the sweetness of a blessed life, meditation perceives it, prayer asks for it, contemplation tastes it. Reading, as it were, puts food whole into the mouth, meditation chews it and breaks it up, prayer extracts its flavor, contemplation is the sweetness itself which gladdens and refreshes.[8]

In the remainder of the work, Guigo explains each stage more fully, with the emphasis on the final stage, contemplation. He is concerned throughout to caution his readers against an aridly rational reading of Scripture. This caution made his work especially popular with the *devotio moderna* movement and resonates with Benedict's own concern that the study of Scripture not become a scholarly enterprise cut off from prayer and personal engagement in faith and love.

In his recapitulation, Guigo emphasizes the causal order of these four stages: *lectio* is the foundation and provides the subject matter; *meditatio* actively digs deeper for the treasure contained within; *oratio* then asks God for the fruits of this treasure that has been found; and *contemplatio* is God's

5. For background to Guigo II and *The Ladder of Monks*, see the introduction to *The Ladder of Monks and Twelve Meditations*, trans. Edmund Colledge and James Walsh (Garden City, NY: Image Books, 1978). For a treatment of Guigo within the history of *lectio divina*, see Laurence Kriegshauser, "Western Monastic Tradition of Lectio Divina and Seminary Formation," 9–30, at 16–17 of the present volume.

6. *The Ladder of Monks* 1, p. 81.

7. *The Ladder of Monks* 2, p. 82.

8. *The Ladder of Monks* 3, pp. 82–83.

answer to this prayer, feeding and inebriating the soul with "the dew of heavenly sweetness."[9] Notably, Guigo echoes Benedict's goal when he states that "if meditation is to be fruitful, it must be followed by devoted prayer, and the sweetness of contemplation may be called the effect of that prayer."[10] Guigo, however, offers little help on linking to Benedict's final stage, *actio*. For the cloistered monk, at least in Guigo's view, "the good works of the active life" are an obstacle to climbing this ladder of four rungs, something to be endured but not embraced.[11]

Guigo may have received the model of these four stages through a personal revelation, but something akin to these stages had already been proposed by Hugh of Saint Victor (d. 1141), whom Guigo clearly read. Notably, Hugh adds a fifth stage to the sequence, *actio*, located between prayer and contemplation.[12] Clearly there was some divergence concerning just how this process of reading and prayer was to be most effectively carried out. Notwithstanding this diversity, the ordering of *lectio divina* into these four discrete stages became popular in the later medieval period. "Prescriptive as well as descriptive, Guigo II's outline anticipates the systematic prayer methods of the following centuries, those that will be summarized in the *Spiritual Exercises* of Ignatius of Loyola."[13] Saint John of the Cross, for example, employs these four stages when teaching his fellow Carmelites.[14]

An online search of these four Latin terms—*lectio*, *meditatio*, *oratio*, *contemplatio*—showed that this fourfold model is widely accepted and employed today by a variety of spiritual traditions: Benedictines, Cistercians, Carmelites, Camaldolese, and Dominicans. Occasionally the origin of these terms in the writings of Guigo II is acknowledged, but often not. The descriptions of the four stages vary somewhat but have a family resemblance. Perhaps the most frequent gloss made by contemporary authors on the four stages urges a modification of Guigo's causal sequence by maintaining that the four stages are *not* necessarily sequential and causative:

9. *The Ladder of Monks* 12, pp. 92–93.

10. *The Ladder of Monks* 13, p. 95.

11. *The Ladder of Monks* 15, p. 97.

12. For the appearance of an ordered process of reading and prayer in the early twelfth century, see Duncan Robertson, *Lectio Divina: The Medieval Experience of Reading* (Collegeville, MN: Liturgical Press, 2011), xvii. See also Jordan Aumann, *Christian Spirituality in the Catholic Tradition* (San Francisco: Ignatius, 1985), 120, for the appearance of these terms in Hugh of Saint Victor.

13. Robertson, *Lectio Divina*, xvii–xviii.

14. Aumann, *Christian Spirituality*, 120.

> Lectio can thus be viewed as a pathway towards contemplation. This is not, however, to say that the four steps constitute a sequential method to be followed, or that each is present in every lectio. Often the various phases are spread throughout the day as mindfulness of the Word is prolonged, and we keep responding to what we have read in the way that we live.[15]

Oratio, Contemplatio, and *Actio* of *Lectio Divina*

What I wish to do now is to return to the text of *Verbum Domini* in order to consider how Benedict XVI conceives of the *oratio, contemplatio,* and *actio* that follow from an exegetically informed *lectio divina.* First a disclaimer: the Catholic tradition on prayer, contemplation, and action is so vast that any attempt even to summarize this massive tradition would quickly run aground.[16] My goal is modest: by considering Benedict's formulations in dialogue with select witnesses from the tradition, I hope to offer concise recommendations for how seminarians today can be formed in this ancient approach to the reading and study of sacred Scripture.

Oratio

Benedict's treatment of the relationship between *lectio* and *oratio* appears in *Verbum Domini,* §86–87. He begins by citing *Dei verbum,* §25, which itself cites Saint Ambrose on the essential interconnection between biblical reading and prayer:

> The Synod Fathers thus took up the words of the Dogmatic Constitution *Dei Verbum*: "Let the faithful go gladly to the sacred text itself, whether in the sacred liturgy, which is full of the divine words, or in devout reading, or in such suitable exercises and various other helps which, with the approval and guidance of the pastors of the Church, are happily spreading everywhere in our day. Let them remember, however, that prayer should accompany the reading of sacred Scripture."[17]

15. Michael Casey, "The Art of Lectio Divina," 106–109 in *The Benedictine Handbook* (Collegeville, MN: Liturgical Press, 2003), 107.

16. For example, the article on "contemplation" runs to more than 450 columns in fine print in the *Dictionnaire de Spiritualité: Ascétique et mystique, doctrine et histoire,* ed. Marcel Viller, Ferdinand Cavallera, and Joseph de Guibert (Paris: Beauchesne, 1953), 1643–2194.

17. *Verbum Domini,* §86, citing *Dei verbum,* §25, and Ambrose, *On the Duties of Ministers,* book 1, chapter 20, section 88. Robertson, *Lectio Divina,* xi, traces this tradition of uniting reading and prayer back to Cyprian of Carthage; it became a principle found in many of the Western Fathers of the Church, including Ambrose, Jerome, and Isidore of Seville.

Benedict then cites texts from Augustine and Origen to the same effect, namely, that prayer ought always to accompany the reading of sacred Scripture.[18] Benedict presents all this as a reappropriation of the patristic manner of reading the Bible that should be undertaken not only as individuals, but also communally, especially in the liturgy of the Mass.

Finally, we come to Benedict's own summation of what it means to follow the *lectio* of Scripture with prayer: "Following this comes prayer (*oratio*), which asks the question: *what do we say to the Lord in response to his word?* Prayer, as petition, intercession, thanksgiving and praise, is the primary way by which the word transforms us."[19] Several things are worthy of notice here. First, prayer (*oratio*) is fundamentally our response to God himself; it is our part of the conversation that God has initiated with us through his word. This accords well with the traditional understanding that recommends a personal, even conversational, prayer in response to what God is revealing. Second, Benedict understands *oratio* to include petition and intercession on the one hand, and thanksgiving and praise on the other. This is a wide notion of prayer, opening up room for varied forms of response. Third and finally, Benedict states that it is through our response in prayer that the word read and meditated upon actually transforms us. Without such prayer, reading and meditation fall short of the transformational purpose of our encounter with the word of God.

Benedict's description of *oratio* has much in common with what we found in Guigo's account. For Guigo as for Benedict, it is prayer that enables the word of God to be genuinely transformative in my life. For Guigo, *oratio* is principally an expression of desire, my desire that the word be fulfilled in me. On this model, *oratio* is primarily petition that the word have its full effect in my life. Yet Benedict's account of *oratio* opens up a broader scope for application than we find in Guigo. Notably, Benedict leaves room for thanksgiving and praise as a proper prayerful response to the word. Not every word of Scripture easily lends itself to personal appropriation: What shall I do? Many passages of the Bible simply glorify God and show the wonder of his works. The appropriate response to this is praise, thanksgiving, and wonder. It is *this* kind of prayer that, on the right occasion, enables the word to transform our hearts.

Importantly, Benedict's inclusion of intercession as part of our response directs prayer to mission, to the impact of the word not just in my life but for others. This I believe is crucial, especially for the priest who is active in

18. *Verbum Domini,* §86. The text from Augustine is from *Enarrationes in Psalmos* 85, section 7; the text from Origen is from *Epistola ad Gregorium* 3.

19. *Verbum Domini,* §87, emphasis in the original.

ministry. This is the *prophetic* aspect of prayer. Often the reading of and meditation upon the word of God draws us to pray that "the flock" would know and be transformed by this word. We become convicted and impassioned by the word, and so ready to preach and proclaim. This is fully in keeping with what we find in Paul's letters where he consistently says that he prays for the churches, asking that the fruits of the Spirit be more and more manifest in the people of God. And so we find three distinct but coordinated avenues for *oratio* that follows upon *lectio*: prayer for oneself, prayer for others, and prayer that expresses praise and thanks to God. Which form of response predominates will depend on what has been read and how the Spirit is moving. And though this *oratio* will often be made in silence, in my experience the prayer of intercession and of praise is best expressed by speaking the prayer aloud.

Contemplatio

Benedict's statement on *contemplatio* focuses on the need for seeing the word from God's point of view and growing in discernment. He begins: "Finally, *lectio divina* concludes with contemplation (*contemplatio*), during which we take up, as a gift from God, his own way of seeing and judging reality, and ask ourselves *what conversion of mind, heart and life is the Lord asking of us?*"[20] This is followed by a citation of Romans 12:2, the call to be transformed in our minds so that we might take on the will and mind of God himself. Benedict then underlines the fruit of discernment that contemplation brings: "Contemplation aims at creating within us a truly wise and discerning vision of reality, as God sees it, and at forming within us 'the mind of Christ' (1 Cor 2:16)." In short, contemplation of the word produces the capability for true discernment. Benedict follows this with a citation from Hebrews 4:12 about the searching and discerning function of the word of God in our lives.[21]

At first blush, this seems to be just another way of describing one aspect of the role of *oratio*, a form of personal petition that the word would have its full and complete effect in me. In one sense, Benedict seems to move away from, or at least to leave unaddressed, the most common way of identifying the particular mark and identifying feature of contemplation, namely, that in contemplation the soul is especially *passive* in the presence of the word of God. In contemplation, as traditionally conceived, God by his grace is especially active, providing the soul with a divine communion beyond all words and images. In the tradition, especially as it developed in the later medieval

20. *Verbum Domini*, §87, emphasis in the original.
21. *Verbum Domini*, §87.

period and beyond, contemplation is marked by the soul abandoning its own efforts, leaving behind words, images, and constructs, and dwelling in God's presence. This kind of orientation is notably missing from Benedict's account of contemplation.

Perhaps Benedict is attempting to sidestep the longstanding debate between ascetical and mystical prayer and the controversies over the nature of contemplation. Whether he is or not, Benedict focuses more on the *results* of contemplation than on its typical mode of operation. And yet connections with a traditional rendering of *contemplatio* are certainly present. It is, first, a gift of God, not something that we can produce by our own efforts. Second, it brings to us God's own view; through contemplation we are enabled to see the way God sees. If *oratio* describes our active response of prayer to God's word, *contemplatio* here seeks and finds God's own view that comes through the word itself searching and discerning our hearts (and changing them).

Still, Benedict's use of the terms "vision" and "seeing" in his description link contemplation more with the intellect (and a result in the intellect) than with the will or the affections. This emphasis is different than we find in Guigo, where contemplation is consistently described in terms of the "sweetness" of God's word beyond any active faculty of the soul. Benedict's emphasis here also stands in notable tension with many popular accounts of contemplation offered today, where contemplation is depicted as non- or anti-intellectual, and as operating primarily in the will and the affections.[22]

While we might wish to modify Benedict's description of *contemplatio* to include a place for communion with God in love that engages the will and affections, I am grateful to Benedict for avoiding the popular anti-intellectual account of contemplation that is common today. If the goal is for seminarians to integrate their biblical studies—including historical-critical exegesis—with a life of prayer, then an account of *lectio divina*, and especially of contemplation, that eschews the intellect and focuses on love and affection *alone* only serves to sharpen and harden the divide that we are seeking to bridge and integrate. There *is* a proper caution to be made against an overly-intellectual approach to both meditation and contemplation that prevents the "heart" from being engaged, but the opposite extreme, shutting down the intellect in order to

22. A contemporary example that leans in this direction is the description of "contemplation" and "contemplative prayer" by William H. Shannon, in *The New Dictionary of Catholic Spirituality*, ed. Michael Downey (Collegeville, MN: Liturgical Press, 1993), 209–214. Shannon says that the heart of contemplation is a focus on love rather than thought. Discursive reason that is active in meditation divides, while contemplative love unites (209).

enter into meditation and especially contemplation, is equally injurious. One could make a case that this is just what in fact did occur in the late medieval period: the reaction to an overly arid scholasticism led to an overly-affective approach to meditation, and the result was a dis-integration of the two.

In my own experience, meditation and contemplation succeed best when I open myself fully to the word, and allow that word—and the Spirit of God at work through that word—to guide both my active meditation and my receptive contemplation of that word. Sometimes in this process, my mind is fully engaged—I am enabled to see in marvelous light some truth or reality, and this "seeing" itself has a transformative effect and naturally gives rise to wonder and thanks. Sometimes my love and affections are engaged, and the result is a conversation with God, or a time of communing with God, that has little intellective content. If we are to bridge the divide between biblical study and prayer, I believe we need to encourage the full activity (and passivity) of the intellect and will in response to the word of God, allowing that word to engage and transform us in all aspects of our being. Here we should note that Benedict concludes his treatment of contemplation by pointing us to Mary the Mother of God as the "supreme synthesis and fulfillment" of the entire process of receiving and contemplating the word of God.[23]

Actio

Pope Benedict's comment on *actio* is brief and seems to be included for completeness, so that the consequences of a fully-fledged *lectio divina* are manifested in action. He writes: "We do well also to remember that the process of *lectio divina* is not concluded until it arrives at action (*actio*), which moves the believer to make his or her life a gift for others in charity."[24] In this case the gift of God given to the believer is meant to result in the gift of one's life in charity for the sake of others. A great deal could be said about the translation of *lectio* into action, but in the brief space afforded here, I would like to point to one aspect of action-inspired biblical reading and study, namely, the fundamental distinction between a restless, anxiety-filled activity on the one hand, and an activity that comes out of and draws from prayer and contemplation on the other.

As we all know, our contemporary culture is hugely biased in favor of *activity*. Even people who claim no spiritual foundation recognize the superficial hyper-activity that characterizes modern life. People are seldom at rest, unable

23. *Verbum Domini*, §87.
24. *Verbum Domini*, §87.

to focus, constantly distracted, and unable to find the *human* space for rest and quiet. We are not a contemplative culture. Given this, we might be tempted to focus solely on meditation, prayer, and contemplation, and leave action to take care of itself. But this would only contribute to a disengagement of contemplation and action, and would abandon to the modern culture the task of defining what a Christian disciple's *actio* should look like.

Instead, we need to see true Christian *actio* as naturally arising from reading, prayer, and contemplation, which together provide the crucial foundation for a faith-filled, humbled, and grounded activity. According to Jordan Aumann, the great teachers of contemplative-active integration are Augustine, Thomas Aquinas, and especially Gregory the Great.[25] I will briefly draw from each one to illustrate how *actio* arises from and returns to *contemplatio*.

As is so often the case, Augustine lays the foundation for understanding how the contemplative and active aspects of Christian life work together. He recognizes that there are states of life that are primarily contemplative or active, but then urges that one of these cannot be emphasized to the abandonment of the other:

> As to these three modes of life, the contemplative, the active, and the composite, although, so long as a man's faith is preserved, he may choose any of them without detriment to his eternal interests, yet he must never overlook the claims of truth and duty. No man has a right to lead such a life of contemplation as to forget in his own ease the service due to his neighbor; nor has any man a right to be so immersed in active life as to neglect the contemplation of God.[26]

Gregory the Great builds his account upon Augustine's foundation. From his own profound experience of living both active and contemplative callings, Gregory repeatedly considers how they mutually strengthen each other (and notably by "contemplation" Gregory seems to include the entire complex of *lectio*, *meditatio*, *oratio*, and *contemplatio* that Benedict proposes). For Gregory, the great exemplar for a contemplative life leading to *actio* and then back to *contemplatio* is Christ himself:

> It is hence that the Redeemer of mankind in the day time exhibits his miracles in cities, and spends the night in devotion to prayer upon the mountain, namely, that he may teach all perfect preachers, that they should neither entirely leave the active life, from love of the speculative, nor wholly slight

25. Aumann, *Christian Spirituality*, 165.

26. Augustine, *City of God*, trans. Marcus Dods, NPNF 2, (Grand Rapids: Eerdmans, 1979), book 19, chapter 19.

> the joys of contemplation from excess in working, but in quiet imbibe by contemplation, what in employment they may pour back to their neighbors by word of mouth. For by contemplation they rise into the love of God, but by preaching they return back to the service of their neighbor.[27]

From Christ's own example of ministry by day and prayer by night, Gregory draws the lesson for Christ's preachers: there must be a back-and-forth, an investment in reading, prayer, and contemplation so that, enflamed with the love of God and his truth, they can offer the fruits of their labor for the good of others.[28]

While Gregory employs the Martha-Mary contrast to exhibit the two states of life, active and contemplative, he more commonly distinguishes and unites the two by referring them to love of neighbor and love of God respectively. This has the distinct advantage of showing how both action and contemplation, though distinct, together fulfill the command of love:

> For holy men, as was said before, are sent and go forth as lightnings, when they come forth from the retirement of contemplation, to the public life of employment. They are sent and they go, when, from the secrecy of inward meditation, they spread forth into the wide space of active life. But they return and say to God, "Here we are," because after the outward works which they perform, they always return to the bosom of contemplation, there to revive the flame of their zeal, and to glow as it were from the touch of heavenly brightness. For they would freeze too speedily amid their outward works, good though they be, did they not constantly return with anxious earnestness to the fire of contemplation.[29]

What Gregory secures here is the contemplative fount from which activity springs. We need not be too idealistic about the rough and tumble nature of active ministry. Christ and his disciples on at least one occasion went off to pray and found themselves pursued by people who insisted on receiving ministry. And Christ gave himself in ministry, even though he had other plans for rest and restoration. The crucial truth to secure is that Christian *actio*, of

27. Gregory the Great, *Moralia* (Oxford: John Henry Parker, 1844), book 6, paragraph 56.

28. Gregory several times elaborates on Christ as the model and exemplar of how the contemplative and active life are meant to be integrated, expressive of both love of God and love of neighbor: "For he is called in one sense 'a corner stone,' because he united in himself two peoples, and in another, because he set forth in himself patterns of both lives, that is, the active and the contemplative, united together. For the contemplative life differs very much from the active. But our Redeemer by coming Incarnate, while he gave a pattern of both, united both in himself" (*Moralia*, 28.33).

29. Gregory, *Moralia*, 30.8. See also 30.48.

whatever kind, is intended to be fueled by nourishment from the word of God and prayer.

We turn to Aquinas on the contemplative and active vocations. Aquinas cites the text from Augustine quoted above and offers this significant comment upon it:

> Sometimes a man is called away from the contemplative life to the works of the active life, on account of some necessity of the present life, yet not so as to be compelled to forsake contemplation altogether. . . . Hence it is clear that when a person is called from the contemplative life to the active life, this is done by way not of subtraction but of addition.[30]

In a wonderful piece of theological exposition, Thomas shows how the active life hinders contemplative activity in one sense but prepares the way for and eases contemplation in another sense:

> The active life may be considered from two points of view. First, as regards the attention to and practice of external works: and thus it is evident that the active life hinders the contemplative, in so far as it is impossible for one to be busy with external action, and at the same time give oneself to Divine contemplation. Secondly, active life may be considered as quieting and directing the internal passions of the soul; and from this point of view the active life is a help to the contemplative, since the latter is hindered by the inordinateness of the internal passions. . . . Hence the work of the active life conduces to the contemplative, by quelling the interior passions which give rise to the phantasms whereby contemplation is hindered.[31]

In a series of audiences following the promulgation of *Verbum Domini*, Benedict himself identifies the tendency to mere activism and points the way for prayer and contemplation of the word of God in Scripture as crucial for charity-informed *actio*:

> Without daily prayer lived with fidelity, our acts are empty, they lose their profound soul, and are reduced to being mere activism which in the end leaves us dissatisfied. . . . Contemplation of God must also be present. We must not lose ourselves in pure activism but always let ourselves also be penetrated in our activities by the light of the word of God and thereby learn true charity, true service to others, which does not need many things—it certainly needs the necessary things—but needs above all our heartfelt

30. Thomas Aquinas, *Summa Theologiae*, II–II, q. 182, a. 1, ad 3, in *Summa Theologica: Complete English Edition in Five Volumes*, vol. 2, trans. Fathers of the English Dominican Province (New York: Benzinger, 1947), 1943–1944.

31. *Summa Theologiae*, II–II, q. 182, a. 3.

> affection and the light of God. . . . Every step in our life, every action, of the Church too, must be taken before God, in the light of his word.[32]

Activity in the world will always partake of challenge and disruption, of unexpected claims that foil our stable patterns of prayer. Saints Augustine, Gregory, and Thomas—and Pope Benedict—show us that, fueled by a prayerful and contemplative reading of Scripture, the servants of God can undertake active, even disruptive, service in the power of Christ, equipped to do God's work, and that in turn this active ministry helps fuel a return to a life-giving *lectio divina*.

32. Benedict XVI, General Audience (April 25, 2012). w2.vatican.va/content/benedict-xvi/en/audiences/2012/documents/hf_ben-xvi_aud_20120425.html.

Exquisitio, Supplicatio, Praedicatio: Searching the Scriptures and the Mystery of Preaching

Anthony Giambrone, OP

Hughes Oliphant Old's imposing seven-volume, 4,500-page opus, *The Reading and Preaching of the Scriptures in the Worship of the Christian Church*, makes one point unmistakably clear.[1] Huge diversity characterizes the Church's long exercise of the ministry of the Word. An immediate and important corollary results: it is a mistake to make any single manner of *lectio* simply normative for the ecclesial reading and preaching of the Scriptures.

The aggressive branding of the familiar, four-step *scala* model of monastic meditation as *lectio divina tout court* represents a special danger in this connection.[2] To accept this monopolistic identification would be to universalize and impose a devotional practice rightly left to the liberty of the faithful, like the *Raccolta*'s once incentivized prayers before and after *Sacrae Scripturae lectio,* e.g., 500 days' indulgence for kissing the Gospels with certain approved invocations.[3]

1. Hughes Oliphant Old, *The Reading and Preaching of the Scriptures in the Worship of the Christian Church,* 7 vols. (Grand Rapids: Eerdmans, 1998, 1998, 1999, 2002, 2004, 2007, 2010).

2. The "rediscovery" and promotion of the four-step model of monastic *lectio divina* represents the most important response to the Second Vatican Council's call for prayerful reading of the Scriptures (cf. *Verbum Domini,* §87). See James Chuckwuma Okoye, *Scripture in the Church: The Synod on the Word of God and the Post-synodal Exhortation Verbum Domini* (Collegeville, MN: Liturgical Press, 2011), 93–104.

3. The many indulgences formerly attached to devout reading of the Scriptures have been simplified in the present *Enchiridion indulgentiarum* (§30, Sacrae Scripturae lectio). The present, streamlined norms read as follows: "§1. *Plenaria indulgentia* conceditur christifideli qui Sacram Scripturam, iuxta textum a competenti auctoritate adprobatum, cum veneratione divino eloquio debita et ad modum lectionis spiritalis, per dimidiam saltem horam legerit; si per minus tempus id egerit *indulgentia* erit *partialis.* §2. Quod si rationabili de causa quis legere non valeat, *indulgentia, plenaria* vel *partialis* prout supra, conceditur, si textus ipse Sacrae Scripturae, vel alio legente vel ope instrumentorum, quae « video » vel « audio » vocantur, percipitur." Apostolic Penitentiary, *Enchiridion indulgentiarum: Normae et concessiones* (Vatican City: Libreria Editrice Vaticana, 1999), p. 75.

Naturally, *The Ladder of Monks*[4] promotes a depth of simplicity and personal engagement in scriptural reading that should in no way be flippantly caricatured or dismissed. It is worth remarking, nevertheless, that nothing in the important, we may add *binding* commendation of scriptural reading and study at the close of *Dei verbum* narrows the project to the ruminative exercise associated with Guigo II.

> Therefore, all the clergy must hold fast to the Sacred Scriptures through diligent sacred reading and careful study (*assidua lectione sacra atque exquisito studio in Scripturis*), especially the priests of Christ and others, such as deacons and catechists, who are legitimately active in the ministry of the word. This cultivation of Scripture is required lest any of them become "an empty preacher of the word of God outwardly, who is not a listener to it inwardly" since they must share the abundant wealth of the divine word with the faithful committed to them, especially in the sacred liturgy. This sacred Synod earnestly and specifically urges all the Christian faithful, especially religious, to learn by frequent reading of the divine Scriptures (*divinarum Scripturarum lectione*) the "excelling knowledge of Jesus Christ" (Phil. 3:8). "For ignorance of the Scriptures is ignorance of Christ." Therefore, they should gladly put themselves in touch with the sacred text itself, whether it be through the liturgy, rich in the divine word, or through devotional reading (*per piam lectionem*), or through instructions suitable for the purpose and other aids which, in our time, are commendably available everywhere, thanks to the approval and active support of the shepherds of the Church. And let them remember that prayer should accompany the reading of sacred Scripture, so that God and man may talk together; for "we speak to Him when we pray; we hear Him when we read the divine sayings."[5]

Quoting Saint Augustine's Sermon 179, the Church simply expresses here her earnest wish that priests and other ministers of the word be not "empty preachers." Rather, by assiduous reading and searching study, they should be truly fit to share with the faithful, above all liturgically, the great treasure entrusted to their care in the sacred text. Prayer is intoned as the enveloping atmosphere

4. For the critical Latin text, see Guigo II, *Lettre sur la vie contemplative (l'échelle des moins) et Douze Méditations*, ed. Edmund Colledge and James Walsh, SC 163 (Paris: Cerf, 1970); see also *Scala Paradisi* (PL 40, 997–1004) and *Scala Claustralium* (PL 184, 475–484). For an English translation, see *The Ladder of Monks and Twelve Meditations*, trans. Edmund Colledge and James Walsh (Garden City, NY: Doubleday, 1978).

5. Second Vatican Council, *Dei verbum* (November 18, 1965), 111–128 in *The Documents of Vatican II*, trans. Joseph Gallagher, ed. Walter M. Abbot (New York: Guild Press, 1966), §25; citing Augustine, Sermon 179, section 1 (PL 38, 966); Jerome, *Commentary on Isaiah*, Prologue (PL 24, 17); Ambrose, *On the Duties of Ministers*, book 1, chapter 20, section 88 (PL 16, 50).

of such reading. The prime objective is increasing the measure and quality of ecclesial contact with the Holy Scriptures.

Such a goal necessarily invites an open approach to the project of reading. Liturgical encounters, private devotional reading, and guided study are all promoted. Here the attitude of generously promoting liberal access to the Scriptures corresponds to a broad conciliar theme, most famously expressed in *Sacrosanctum Concilium*: "The treasures of the Bible are to be opened up more lavishly, so that richer fare may be provided for the faithful at the table of God's Word" (§51).[6]

Dining lavishly on the rich fare of this sacred table is not a new ecclesial ideal, cramped as the Church's praxis admittedly was for a certain season. In just this respect, we should carefully avoid misperceptions about the spirit of the so-called "counter-reformation," however. It is of high interest to observe, for instance, that at the very origin of modern priestly formation as it was crafted in the 1570s–80s under the visionary headship of William Cardinal Allen at the first Tridentine seminary, the English College at Douay, the seminarians feasted on three to five chapters of Scripture as the table reading at each of their two daily meals. In this way, the students heard the entire Old Testament read through twelve times and the New Testament a full sixteen times in the course of just three years.[7] Such coverage and quantity of reading presents an apostolically oriented model of *lectio* at the other pole from the cloistered *scala* method, where monks spent an entire year occupied with a single book, assigned to them by the abbot, slowly sucking the sweetness from single words as from savory morsels.

The extraordinary ingestion of scripture at Douay actually goes farther, for each student cycled through a second course, also daily reading privately in his room the passages read publicly in the refectory, preferably in the original language—an exercise, quite frankly, that would mortify most contemporary doctoral students in biblical studies. To this already ambitious program of reading, we may also add daily lectures on the New Testament and a systematic treatment of controverted scriptural texts, outlining the Catholic interpretation and confuting the Protestant side. In this vein, there was likewise a weekly disputation, students being trained not only to argue the Catholic view, but in

6. Second Vatican Council, *Sacrosanctum Concilium* (December 4, 1963), 137–178 in *The Documents of Vatican II*, trans. Joseph Gallagher, ed. Walter M. Abbot (New York: Guild Press, 1966), §51.

7. On Allen and the seminary at Douay, see Eamon Duffy, *Reformation Divided: Catholics, Protestants and the Conversion of England* (London: Bloomsbury, 2017), 132–167.

good dialectic fashion to understand the opposing case as well by defending it themselves and advancing hostile objections. Twice each week, finally, some student would offer a scriptural sermon on one or other of the controverted points.

In what follows, I would like to take this remarkable model of early-modern seminary formation as the starting point for my reflection on the intertwining themes of study, *lectio*, and preaching. As a model for the *assidua lectione sacra atque exquisito studio in Scripturis* called for by *Dei verbum,* I find Douay an excellent challenge to our own postconciliar zeal and institutional imagination. The half-millennium that now separates us from the Reformation is a considerable distance, however, and Bible reading in our day has become considerably more complicated. As a second postulate and point of departure, therefore, I would also like to add an experiential datum, an observation that inculpates my own discipline of exegesis in an embarrassing way. In the recent words of Pope Benedict,

> Anyone today who reads the ever-thicker commentaries on the Gospels remains disappointed in the end. He learns a lot that is useful about those days and a lot of hypotheses that ultimately contribute nothing at all to an understanding of the text. In the end you feel that in all the excess of words, something essential is lacking: entrance into Jesus's silence, from which his word is born. If we cannot enter this silence, we will always hear the word only on its surface and thus not really understand it.[8]

The disappointment Benedict mentions is more than just a frustration; it is an interpretative, and therefore evangelical, calamity. Leo XIII spoke memorably of "writers who, being without the true faith, only gnaw the bark of the Sacred Scripture, and never attain its pith" (*Providentissmus Deus,* §15).[9] When such writers assert their own monopoly on *lectio*, as they do in most seminary classrooms, the "empty preachers" Augustine feared will inevitably fill the pulpits. No one has taught them how "to pierce the pearl," to quote my own professor of homiletics.[10]

8. Pope Benedict XVI, afterword to Robert Cardinal Sarah, *The Power of Silence: Against the Dictatorship of Noise* (San Francisco: Ignatius, 2017), 243.

9. Pope Leo XIII, *Providentissmus Deus* (November 18, 1893), 37–61 in *The Scripture Documents: An Anthology of Official Catholic Teachings,* trans. P. Dean Béchard (Collegeville, MN: Liturgical Press, 2002), §15, p. 50 (no. 32 in Béchard's numbering).

10. See Peter John Cameron, *Why Preach? Encountering Christ in God's Word* (San Francisco: Ignatius, 2007).

I do not perceive anything today quite so obtuse as the learned, late medieval sermons against which the Reformers railed; still the pedantic irrelevance of most contemporary scriptural science leads directly into a kerygmatic cul-de-sac. Without sounding another modernist alarm, the patent disbelief of a very large measure of this scholarship must also be frankly acknowledged. To this degree, enlightened demythologizing continues to worm its way into the minds of the ministers of the word to the grave detriment of Church life. Any product of preaching that stems from too strict a regimen of such commentary reading—and this includes anti-intellectual counterreactions—slaves under an academic superego that must in the end stifle the audible authority of Christ's Church. The irony is that as the living voice of Christ thus vanishes, the resulting void offers no refuge of true silence, only the prophesied plague of a famine for God's word (Amos 8:11).[11]

Precisely here, Benedict's stress on the recovery of Christian silence exposes another embarrassment, however: dilettantism. The evident attachment of the postconciliar Church to the practice of monastic *lectio divina* as a privileged means of ecclesial renewal risks underwriting an evident superficiality.[12] If one takes with real seriousness the ascetical rigor that structured Guigo's twelfth-century Carthusian life—the saturating solitude, the frightful penance, the full immersion in liturgy and nature—it should increase our distant respect for the four grades of spiritual ascension he fell upon one day during his manual labor.[13] Indeed, if this is the native spiritual habitat and proper context for his *scala claustralium*, simple honesty obliges us to recall the abyss dividing the appreciation from the assimilation of a tradition. For the danger goes well beyond indulging the sort of erudite aestheticism of a Benedictine oblate like J.-K. Huysmans.[14] We risk trivializing monastic silence and its mystical ascent

11. The *glossa ordinaria* at 1 Macc 9:24 ("In those days there was a very great famine") reads: "By a lack of preaching, on account of a famine for the word of God." *Biblia Latina cum Glossa Ordinaria: Facsimile Reprint of the Editio Princeps, Adolph Rusch of Strassburg 1480/81*, vol. 3, *Isaias . . . I–II Maccabaeorum* (Turnhout, Belgium: Brepols, 1992), 485.

12. See, e.g., *Verbum Domini*, §87 and Benedict XVI's 2005 address commemorating the 40th anniversary of *Dei verbum*. See also Okoye, *Scripture in the Church*, 94.

13. Guigo II, *The Ladder of Monks* 2, "Cum die quadam corporali manuum labore occupatus de spiritali hominis exercitio cogitare coepissem, quatuor spiritales gradus animo cogitanti se subito obtulerunt, lectio scilicet, meditation, oratio, contemplatio," Colledge and Walsch, *L'échelle des moins*, pp. 84–86. The orientation of the entire exercise toward monastic perfection is suggested by Guigo's considered choice of *Beati mundo corde* as the verse for illustration. Cf. Boniface Ramsey, *John Cassian, The Conferences*, ACW 57 (New York: Newman Press, 1997), 35–76.

14. J.-K. Huysmans, *L'Oblat* (Paris: Stock, 1903).

as we trivialize Gregorian chant, when we make it background music for our morning commute.

At stake in all this is the pressing, contemporary search for a reintegrated experience of the Holy Scriptures, that philosopher's stone that continues to elude us. By some alchemy of postmodern Catholic genius, the corporate enterprise of historical exegesis must be melded with a contemplative praxis of liturgical reading and personal *lectio pia*, blending intelligence and devotion as the ecclesial recipe for some more convicting kergymatic fruit. Beginning with Benedict and *Verbum Domini,* to Pope Francis's effort in *Evangelii gaudium* and the Vatican's new directory on preaching, many useful things have been said already. There is, nevertheless, always room for annotation and new audacity. Let us, then, return to Douay.

The formidable scale of the scriptural formation at the English seminary in exile obviously represents a direct and aggressive response to pastoral challenges posed by the Reformation. Allen was outfitting a Catholic clergy to meet and overcome Bible-thumping Protestants on their own textual ground. The missionary results of such intellectual equipment might be measured in the magnificent apologetic confidence of Campion's Brag.[15] Geared as it thus was towards the making of martyrdom-bound storm troopers out of the secular clergy, the imposing *ratio studiorum* at Douay nevertheless also stands in strong continuity with an earlier culture of ecclesiastical study. The balanced diet of *lectura* and *disputatio,* specifically, was no invention of early modernity, but the humanistic extension of a long familiar medieval system. These two exercises, Bible reading and debate, in fact, represent the most primitive division in theological science as it emerged in university culture of the 1230s, when a specialized exegesis first began to separate off from a self-conscious discipline of dogmatic reflection. And yet, the point of reference in both domains remained emphatically the same. Very simply, Holy Scripture *was* the curriculum. It

15. Saint Edmund Campion was one of Allen's prize pupils at Douay. His spectacular boast swells with the huge assurance of an expert scriptural debater: "Yet have I such courage in avouching the majesty of Jesus my King, and such affiance in his gracious favor, and such assurance in my quarrel, and my evidence so impregnable, and because I know perfectly that no one Protestant, nor all the Protestants living, nor any sect of our adversaries (howsoever they face men down in pulpits, and overrule us in their kingdom of grammarians and unlearned ears) can maintain their doctrine in disputation. I am to sue most humbly and instantly for combat with all and every of them, and the most principal that may be found: protesting that in this trial the better furnished they come, the better welcome they shall be." See the wonderful account of Evelyn Waugh, *Edmund Campion: A Life* (San Francisco: Ignatius, 2012), and Appendix 1, "Campion's Brag."

was the sole textbook and unrivalled heart of theological study. This obtains as much for sixteenth-century Douay as for thirteenth-century Paris. There is nothing abstract here in making the Bible the "soul of theology."

The organic link binding reading and disputation is very important. Indeed, certain commendably bold recent efforts in Europe to recapture scripture as the soul of Catholic seminary education, have perhaps invited an anti-scholastic eclecticism that ultimately disintegrates the broad coherence and pastoral utility of the project. In this regard, it is of high significance that the literary origins of the scholastic *quaestio,* which we associate with the synthetic rhetoric of a theological *summa,* are actually located in medieval biblical commentaries.[16] Anyone picking up Aquinas' *Lectura supra epistolam ad Romanos,* for instance, will breeze along quite nicely through the first two lectures before suddenly slamming into a disputed question on predestination at Romans 1:4.[17] The same material appears as the sixth question of Thomas's contemporaneous *De Veritate.*[18] The trigger, however, is not in the neat schema of that orderly, speculative account, but in Paul's ad hoc use of the pregnant word ὅριζω, *predestinare* in the Vulgate. In this way, *lectio* gives birth to *disputatio,* or exegesis to theology, if you prefer.

In the highly polemical context of the recusant English Church, of course, the burning scriptural questions disputed at Douay were born of a living engagement with real opponents. An irenic schoolroom exercise in abstraction might thus seem somehow superfluous, ingenious as the objections and *sed contra* might well be. It would be very wrong to consider this a decadent fancy, however. On the contrary, the scholastic tradition betrays on the whole a truly startling immediacy. Thomas's exegetical question is not the historico-linguistic riddle of how to gloss the Greek word for "predestination" in light of its first-century context, but how to describe and understand the reality that word signifies. Such prompt contact with the underwriting mystery, with the salvific *res,* manifests an approach to the Scriptures that Matthew Levering

16. In fact, "all the scholastic literary forms—*quaestio, disputatio, summa, articulus*—arose from the activity of lecturing on a text," Jeremy Holms, "Aquinas' *Lectura in Matthaeum,*" in Thomas Weinandy and Daniel Keating, eds., *Aquinas on Scripture: An Introduction to His Biblical Commentaries* (London: T&T Clark, 2005), 90.

17. Aquinas, *Lectura supra epistolam ad Romanos,* caput 1, lectio 3, pp. 10–13 in *S. Thomae Aquinatis: Super epistolas S. Pauli lectura,* ed. Raphael Cai, vol. 1 of 2 (Taurini: Marietti, 1953).

18. Aquinas, *Quaestiones disputatae de veritate,* question 6, 173–195 in *Opera Omnia,* tome 22, vol 1 (Rome: Editori di San Tommaso, 1975).

has called participatory exegesis.[19] Metaphysical involvement in the divine mechanics of salvation is the grounding premise; and on this premise, a shared soteriological conviction binds the diverse reading cultures of Douay and Paris. The core question at the root of every debate was always the same and never far to find: *How does God offer us his salvation?*

The skill of unfolding in ever-new directions this grand and all-underwriting question is the key that unlocks a true ecclesial reading. Pope Benedict, in his presentation of monastic *lectio*,[20] thus fittingly translates the four steps into four guiding questions: *Lectio:* What does the biblical text say in itself? *Meditatio:* What does the biblical text say to us? *Oratio:* What do we say to the Lord in response to his word? *Contemplatio:* What conversion of mind, heart, and life is the Lord asking of us? The culminating transformation of these questions into the *actio* of charity marks the soteriological orientation of the exercise. A certain existential pressure must hold the reading's questioning accountable, for it concerns our real salvation.

The disciplined posing of questions to the sacred text as a religious exercise has a very long pedigree, of course. The Alexandrian catechetical school deserves mention, above all, in this connection. Not unlike the Jewish Beth Midrash, this school fostered a robust ethos of study as worship, with a rare fusion of accents at once scholastic, mystical, and homiletic. Against this background, Origen, in his *Letter to Gregory*, offers a striking counsel on the piety of diligently searching the Scriptures:

> Apply yourself to the reading of the divine Scriptures (τῇ τῶν θείων γραφῶν ἀναγνώσει); but really apply yourself. For those who read divine things need great application, so that we might not say or think anything rash. Thus applying yourself to sacred reading (τῇ τῶν θείων ἀναγνώσει) with faith (μετὰ πιστῆς) and in a manner pleasing to God, knock when the door is closed and it will be opened to you by that gatekeeper of whom Jesus said, "The gatekeeper will open it for him" (John 10:3). By applying yourself to *lectio divina* (τῇ θείᾳ ἀναγνώσει), search correctly (ὀρθῶς ζήτει) and with unwavering faith in God (μετὰ πίστεως εἰς θεὸν ἀκλινοῦς) for that understanding of the divine Scriptures, which is hidden to many (τὸν κεκρυμμένον τοῖς πολλοῖς νοῦν). Do not be satisfied merely with knocking and seeking: for prayer (ἡ εὐχή) to understand the things of God is likewise absolutely necessary. For this reason, the Savior told us not only: "Seek and

19. Matthew Levering, *Participatory Biblical Exegesis: A Theology of Biblical Interpretation* (Notre Dame: University of Notre Dame, 2008).

20. Pope Benedict XVI, *Verbum Domini*, §87.

> you will find," and "Knock and it shall be opened to you," but also added, "Ask and you shall receive."[21]

In this authoritative exhortation to scriptural study—which carries the huge weight of an indefatigable researcher and preacher—Origen makes two moves that are worth highlighting. First, he insists that the restless inquiry of *anagnōsis* must be conducted in a firm spirit of faith. The reader's determined intellectual quest for knowledge is thus elevated to the level of a supernatural hunger. The questioning of genuine *lectio* must accordingly be calibrated to this order of illumination, led on by the *lumen fidei*. If the quest terminates in human pedantry, as in the sort of commentaries Benedict cites, penned by the πολλοί who never reach the pith, it is an abortive act of reading and wasted industry, a labor which has left the bulk of the true work undone.

Second, in Origen's presentation, the questioning born of reading, beyond the mere intellective act of searching (*midrash*), takes on the distinct modality of prayer. The questioner begins a dialogue with God, interiorly transforming and reorienting the very act of asking. Christian gnosis at this point again diverges from any natural quest for knowledge, grafted though it is upon a kind of philosophical piety.[22] No one denies the evident Neoplatonic imprint or the stages of contemplative ascent in Origen's oeuvre. Nevertheless, I would underscore the humble petitionary nature of his *oratio*. This is not the devotional procedure of a Plotinus. Origen's two-step *lectio divina*—which I take to be very close to the mind of the Church expressed in *Dei verbum*—entails the pursuit of no psychological state, only a twin theological transformation of the scientific impulse of asking.

An illustration of the transition from *lectio* to *oratio* will be helpful. It is not the image of sitting still in a comfortable chair with a Bible opened on your lap, eyes closed and next to a scented candle. It is Saint Thomas Aquinas, another reader of Scripture well-conformed to the mind of the Church, who, when he came to a passage in the Scriptures that he could not understand, would turn to vigils of prayer and fasting, imploring God on high to give him light.[23] The scene may seem exceptional, but it is seems to me the correct image for Origen's simple *lectio-oratio* axis, which we might strengthen and call the *exquisitio-supplicatio* model.

21. Origen, *Epistola ad Gregorium* 3 (PG 11, 92), translation mine.

22. Heidegger's lapidary phrase is apropos: *Das Fragen ist die Frömmigkeit des Denkens,* "Questioning is the piety of thinking."

23. See Marie-Dominique Chenu, *Aquinas and His Role in Theology* (Collegeville, MN: Liturgical Press, 2002), 35.

The force of this formula lies in its animated inflection: "animated" in the etymological sense of the *anima* exercising its powers. Sacred reading in the shape of *exquisitio*, in other words, implies an active application of the mind's faculty of reasoning through inquiry, investigation, and research. It is not a lazy ingestion of biblical language, but an active intellectual engagement with the reality revealed. The surpassing depth of this reality, in turn, which ultimately leads the soul to the mystery of God and his grace, inevitably confronts the questioning reader with his own native limits, moreover. From this depth is born the soul's cry or *supplicatio*: an encompassing confession of personal weakness and divine greatness; an urgent desire for truth and opening of the human spirit to the Holy Spirit's direct instruction. The drama of this dynamic need not register in an emotionally extravagant way. Nevertheless, it is this process of opening the spirit to the same Spirit in which the Scriptures were written that opens not only the mind but also the mouth to be filled with the word whose power is lacking in the ministry of "empty preachers."

Here, then, is a suggestion and a very concrete challenge. Preaching must begin in this primitive and even desperate state of theological questioning. If seminarians are not formed to experience a lively mental and spiritual energy when they contact and read the biblical text, if they foster no inquisitive impulse, no ready and active wonder before the saving mystery, if, in a word, they feel no *eros*, no drive to search in dogged diligence and to ask in pious prayer, then our efforts at forming effective ministers of the Word have failed. Their homilies will only transmit their own boredom to the people. Preachers must somehow be brought to love the Bible—and to love the Bible not just with their affections, but with their minds.

"Theology as a church discipline ought in all its branches to be nothing other than sermon preparation."[24] This oracular comment of Karl Barth puts preaching in the existential place of *actio* and is perhaps typical of Neo-Orthodox interests. It echoes, nevertheless, a telling medieval perspective. For the ontogenesis is not complete in passing from scriptural reading to suppliant converse with God. This word exchanged between God and the soul is ultimately meant to pass into the Church. Thus, at Douay, reading and disputation terminated in exercises of preaching. The progression, again, is of older vintage. In Peter the Chanter's *Verbum abbreviatum*, a late twelfth-century manual for preachers, we first find the triad that was to become a standard medieval sequence: *lectio, disputatio, praedicatio.*

24. Karl Barth, *Homiletics* (Louisville: Westminster John Knox, 1991), 17.

> Engaging with scripture requires three elements: reading, disputation, and preaching . . . Reading is, as it were, the foundation and basement for what follows, for through it the rest is achieved. Disputation is the wall in this building of study, for nothing is fully understood or faithfully preached, if it is not first chewed over by the tooth of disputation. Preaching, which is supported by both of the former, is the roof, sheltering the faithful from the heat and wind of temptation. So we should preach after, not before, the reading of Scripture and the investigation of doubtful matters by disputation.[25]

Praedicatio is the highest form of exegesis, to which the process of searching forms an indispensable preliminary. But what precisely is this culminating interpretative act of preaching? And how does it spring forth from the personal dialogue with God's Word that forms its prologue? Let me first answer with one cautionary word, then conclude with two positive marks that characterize the act of preaching.

First, then, a word of warning: preaching is a grace and a grace of a very particular and mysterious order, for it is a kind of institutionalized charisma, a *gratia gratis data* aligned somehow with the apostolic/episcopal *munus*. The early Friars Preachers, formal cooperators in the bishops' preaching office, thus found themselves in a theoretically awkward and ultimately hopeless position in trying to discern concretely whether the *gratia praedicationis* had been conferred on this or that brother. There was skepticism, for instance, about a certain German friar who preferred prayer to study.[26] (How things in Germany have changed.) Yet, Humbert of Romans saw equally well that "there are and always have been many people who are very well educated, and have applied themselves with great diligence to obtain the grace of preaching, yet they have never succeeded in it."[27] Dominic himself was remembered to have said he studied for his sermons in "the book of charity more than the books of men."[28] In the end, then, the passage to preaching was accorded when a brother was adequately prepared in study, observance, and charity; and Dominican life itself was deemed and devised to be the most apt remote preparation for preaching.[29] This is as far as the channeling of Spirit-given prophecy can go.

25. Cited in Beryl Smalley, *The Study of the Bible in the Middle Ages* (Notre Dame: University of Notre Dame, 1964), 208. See also Gilbert Dahan, "Exégèse et prédication au Moyen Âge," *Revue des sciences philosophiques et théologiques* 95, no. 3 (2011): 557–579.

26. *Vitae Fratrum*, §IV, 5.

27. Humbert of Romans, *Treatise on the Formation of Preachers*, §79, trans. Simon Tugwell in *Early Dominicans: Selected Writings* (New York: Paulist, 1982), 203–204.

28. *Vitae Fratrum*, §II, 25.

29. On the other hand, Humbert also offers the following: "Though a grace of preaching is strictly had by God's gift, a sensible preacher still ought to do what he can to ensure that his

If preaching is thus a charismatic endowment and a *munus*, it marks a formal break with the operations of *lectio* and *oratio*, however much these are conducted under the guidance of the Holy Spirit in the light of faith. A new ecclesiological dimension opens up within the interpretative process, and it is just this ecclesial orientation and character that is the first positive mark of preaching. In *praedicatio* all is elevated: the preparatory sequence of searching is recapitulated on a corporate liturgical level through lectionary readings and ritual prayers, then crowned with a tropological and anagogical realization.[30] Preaching is an eschatological event, a mode of understanding God's revelation nearer to the heavenly *scientia beati*. The *totus Christus* now becomes the living agent of *lectio divina*.

Though raised to his post only by a canonical mandate—"And how can people preach unless they are sent" (Rom 10:15 NABRE)—the preacher's private reading should also make his soul receptive for this ecclesial expansion and elevation. The danger of idiosyncrasy must accordingly be flagged and countered. This means the cultivation of what the tradition calls an *anima ecclesiastica*. So, it may be interesting as an exercise to ask what words in the text caught my attention, but unless I reduce this epiphenomenon of my personal psychology to some deeper theological root, my reading will remain ordered to subjective preoccupations and a self-centered praxis of preaching.

Lectio in its scholastic form by contrast was "a thoroughly communal" venture, a "tradition of inquiry that stretches back in time."[31] It is important somehow to recapture this, if private reading is to lead to preaching. Cardinal Sarah captures it beautifully:

> *Lectio divina* is a great river that carries all the riches accumulated over the course of Church history by the fervent readers of God's Word. *Lectio divina* is never solely our own reading. It feeds on the interpretations of those who have preceded us.[32]

As one of the tributaries to this river, modern commentaries should also shape a priest's *lectio divina*, for there is nothing unholy in asking the questions they

preaching is commendable, by carefully studying what he has to preach." *Treatise on the Formation of Preachers*, §82.

30. "Les quatre sens ne sont pas a mettre au même niveau: la tropologie et l'anagogie doivent être isolées des démarches explicatives et interprétatives. Leur statut est fondamentalement diffèrent de celui de la lettre et de l'Allégorie. Muni de cette clé de lecture, il parait plus facile de justifier la place la tropologie. Comme prolongement de l'exégèse et ouverture du commentaire a la prédication." Dahan, "Exégèse et Prédication," 577.

31. Nicholas Healy, "Introduction," in *Aquinas on Scripture*, 12.

32. Sarah, *The Power of Silence*, 240.

pose—certainly not for an *exquisitio* model with its inquisitive *Frömmigkeit* and hungry power of assimilation. It is pride, in fact, Augustine says, to presume to understand the Scriptures without such mental labor.[33] Still, one must navigate carefully to hold to the main way, for these texts often also finally flow off from the great moving mass of Tradition. The high utility of this imperfectly objective science is, nevertheless, not to be gainsaid. It can clarify the sense of a thousand obscurities with marvelous success and thus channel the mind to more penetrating insights.

As an effective negative control on the literal sense, professional exegesis must not, for all that, sanctimoniously negate the *sensus plenior*, that great ocean of spiritual meaning to which all *lectio* flows. The more decisive negative control is thus the *regula fidei*, and arriving at the spiritual sense must be considered the indispensable goal. The questions animating a priest's personal midrash should accordingly be deeply informed by a knowledge of the history of ecclesial questions and debates, including the reception history of specific passages. The particular value of studying *catenae* and the writings of the Fathers cannot be overstated as a means of enriching private *lectio* with the fertile deposit of the faith. As transcripts of episcopal preaching in its widest, magisterial sense, the Fathers' words have carved out the broad riverbed of the Tradition. Their words must continue, therefore, to shape the words of their presbyteral coworkers. It was no sign of an indigent Church that the sermons of the Fathers were in many times and places simply read out from the pulpit. Humbert has some very honest remarks on this point.[34]

We should not fail to notice here the instructive pattern the Church herself offers. The liturgical *officium lectionis* constantly pairs scriptural and magisterial, usually patristic, texts.[35] The integration of authorities, moreover, of Scripture and Tradition, was the essential substance and structure of scholastic disputation. Such twinning should thus be taken as normative in a fully developed practice of *lectio divina*.

33. Augustine, *De doctrina Christiana*, prologue, paragraphs 5–9.

34. "There are some preachers who do not have the mental capacity to produce decent sermons themselves, but who will not stoop to studying what other people have said, insisting on saying only what they can discover for themselves. They are like people who insist on providing only bread that they have made themselves, even though they are not good bakers . . . Then again there are others who are quite clever and intelligent enough, but who are so confident in their own cleverness that they ignore the saints' comments on Holy Scripture and rely on their own exegesis." *Treatise on the Formation of Preachers*, §91–92.

35. *The Liturgy of the Hours*, 4 vols. (New York: Catholic Book Publishing Co., 1975).

Preaching is ecclesial. It is also effective. This is the second and final mark I wish to underline. Preaching enjoys, at least from a Thomistic perspective, a mode of instrumental agency closely analogous to a sacrament, *quasi quodam instrumento.*[36] It produces effects, in other words, that exceed its own proper power, namely, effects that are greater than the power of a human orator enlightened by faith. This is why a homily on the Passion, for instance, might work to inspire a listener to consecrate his life to Christ in religious vows, though nothing at all touching this topic had been said. Causality properly speaking and more than a coincidental occasionalism is at work here.

The homily, of course, is not a frozen formula like the words of consecration, with *ex opera* ritual efficacy (although the urgent need for a sermonic genre should be stressed).[37] The preacher's affinity is rather with the inspired authors of Scripture, who, illumined by a *lumen propheticum* yet emphatically *veri auctores,* intend and create the text's literal sense with full authorial freedom, but who also serve as the instrument of a surpassing and divinely intended spiritual meaning. This means, specifically, that the preacher must open himself to non-intended meanings in the scriptural text—that is, meanings attributable directly to the divine *auctor* and not circumscribed by historical, human instruments. Yet, to dispose himself to serve a higher agency in this way the preacher, like the inspired prophet, must cooperate with the divine *afflatus.* In authoring and crafting his own proper discourse the preacher must, as in celebrating the sacraments, intend what the Church intends if he is to open his own message to a similar spiritual sense, i.e., the rich moral, Christological, and anagogical meanings that the People of God hear in his words, without his ever suspecting or conniving.

And what the Church intends is both instruction and worship, a simultaneous exercise of the teaching and sanctifying *munera*:

36. See *Summa theologiae* II–II, q. 177, a. 1. For this entire paragraph, see Benoît-Dominique de la Soujeole, "Le mystère de la prédication," *Revue thomiste* 107, no. 3 (2007): 355–374.

37. Naturally, sermonic genres must be adapted to times and places, and Pope Francis's suggested model—an idea, a sentiment, an image—will do much to aid preaching if well applied. I would, nevertheless, like to draw particular attention to the sparkling intelligence of the thirteenth-century *sermo modernus* and its highly effective use of the arts of memory. It is equally succinct as the rhetoric proposed by Francis (and as catching once the procedure is understood). In the practice of the *divisio textus,* moreover, this style adopts a technique of textual analysis that bridges the gap between exegesis and preaching. See Randall B. Smith, *Reading the Sermons of Thomas Aquinas: A Beginner's Guide,* Renewal within Tradition (Steubenville, OH: Emmaus Academic, 2016).

> By means of the homily the mysteries of the faith and the guiding principles of the Christian life are expounded from the sacred text (*Sacrosanctum Concilium*, §52).
>
> Because the homily is an integral part of the liturgy, it is not only an instruction, it is also an act of worship. When we read the homilies of the Fathers, we find that many of them concluded their discourse with a doxology and the word "Amen": they understood that the purpose of the homily was not only to sanctify the people, but to glorify God (*Homiletic Directory*, §4).[38]

These twin dogmatic and doxological ends of the homily should orient the preacher's *lectio divina*. Searching study should lead both to the answers of doctrine and dissolve in silent awe before the majestic surfeit of meaning.

In its liturgical framework the homily prepares for the people's *Credo*. The homilist's task is thus to propose the saving mysteries for the people's assent and worship. His hearers should be moved to respond to his words with a resonating "Yes!" In eliciting this *Amen*, full of contentment and desire, the preacher stands finally in service of the altar.[39] The preacher disposes the confessing faithful to receive Christ sacramentally in spirit and in flesh. The priest's word causes both the mind of Christ and Christ's Body to be made present, drawing men to God and God to men. An anagogical trajectory thus leads his ministry to its goal. The final act of understanding is indeed the sweetness and savor of experience as Guigo said: beyond *lectio*, *oratio*, and *praedicatio*, it belongs to *communicatio* to taste the reality of the spiritual sense.

38. Congregation for Divine Worship, *Homiletic Directory* (Vatican City: Libreria Editrice Vaticana, 2014), §4, p. 1.

39. "It is because the homily is an integral part of the Church's worship that it is to be delivered only by bishops, priests, or deacons. So intimate is the bond between the table of the Word and the table of the altar that it is fitting that 'The Homily should be given by the priest celebrant himself' (*General Instruction of the Roman Missal* 66), or, in any case, always by one ordained to preside or assist at the altar." *Homiletic Directory*, §5.

Contributors

Scott Carl, Saint Paul Seminary School of Divinity, University of St. Thomas, St. Paul, MN

Anthony Giambrone, OP, École Biblique et Archéologique Française de Jérusalem, Israel

Daniel Keating, Sacred Heart Major Seminary, Detroit, MI

Marcin Kowalski, John Paul II Catholic University of Lublin, Poland

Laurence Kriegshauser, OSB, St. Louis Abbey, St. Louis, MO

Michael Magee, Saint Charles Borromeo Seminary, Wynnewood, PA

Konrad Schaefer, OSB, Universidad Pontificia de México, Mexico City, Mexico

Kevin Zilverberg, Saint Paul Seminary School of Divinity, University of St. Thomas, St. Paul, MN

Index of Names and Subjects

Index of Scripture References